The brave adventures of a shoemaker's boy

Ivana Brlić Mažuranić

The brave adventures of a shoemaker's boy

English version by Lorna Wood
based on a translation by
Theresa Mravintz and Branko Brusar

J M Dent & Sons Limited London

First published in Great Britain 1971

Title of the original edition in the Croatian language *Čudnovate zgode šegrta Hlapića*

Made in Great Britain at the
Aldine Press Letchworth Hertfordshire
for J M Dent & Sons Limited
Aldine House Bedford Street London
ISBN 0 460 05752 9

Contents

Ivana Brlić Mažuranić
1874-1938

Loved in her own country as the 'Croatian Andersen', Ivana Mažuranić, born in Ogulin, was a granddaughter of the eminent Ivan Mažuranić, Croatian *ban* (viceroy in the Austro-Hungarian empire) and the author of the greatest Croatian epic poem, *The Death of Smail-Aga Čengić*. At eighteen Ivana married into the old Brlić family at Slavonski Brod. In her autobiography she says: 'When my small band of children began to grow, and when they began to want to read, I felt at once that here was where inclination and duty became one, for I longed to be a writer.'

Her best-known works are *Croatian Tales of Long Ago* (published in London in 1924 and subsequently in twelve other European countries) and *The Brave Adventures of a Shoemaker's Boy*.

In Yugoslavia today, everyone from school age upward knows and loves Lapitch, the small hero of *The Brave Adventures*. The work has been translated into many languages as well as dramatized and produced on the stage, radio and television. The shoemaker's shop can still be seen in Slavonski Brod, and the author's old home, much as it was in her time, is visited every year by hosts of people, young and old, who have enjoyed reading the brave adventures of Lapitch.

At
Master Scowler's

Lapitch the apprentice

Once upon a time there was a little shoemaker's apprentice who had neither father nor mother. His name was Lapitch.

He was small for his twelve years and as cheerful as a bird. He wore ragged trousers and a red shirt and all day long he sat on a three-legged stool driving nails into shoes and sewing them up. And all day long he whistled and sang at his work.

Lapitch's master was called Scowler and he was wicked and frightening. He was so tall that his head came up to the ceiling beams. His hair was like a lion's mane and his moustaches came down to his shoulders. His voice was so strong and deep that when he spoke it sounded like a bear's growl.

Once, in his past life, Master Scowler had tasted great sorrow and misfortune and ever since then he had been very hard-hearted. What had happened to him? That will be told later in the story.

Master Scowler was not only hard-hearted, he was unjust. Whenever he was vexed he cursed Lapitch and shouted at him.

But his wife was sweet and gentle. She had experienced the same sorrow as her husband, but she had a kind heart, and sorrow made her even kinder than before. She loved Lapitch very much.

But even she was afraid of Master Scowler. Whenever she gave Lapitch a piece of fresh bread she smuggled it to him under her apron, so that her husband should not see it. Lapitch loved fresh bread, she knew, but what the master allowed him was always stale and as hard as stone.

Lapitch had only one pair of tattered working-trousers, but Mistress Scowler had made another pair for him for Sundays out of some green cloth. The cloth was a piece left over from Master Scowler's apron and he had told his wife to use it for Lapitch. When the boy put these trousers on he felt like a green frog and he wished he didn't have to

wear them because all the other apprentices in the town made fun of him. But his master said he must wear them on Sundays. Lapitch was always cheerful so when he saw that there was no help for it he pretended to croak every time he put them on. When the other apprentices saw him making a joke of it they stopped teasing him and played with him. He became very popular. But Master Scowler did not like to see Lapitch enjoying himself and always packed him off home when he found him playing games with his friends.

So Lapitch lived at Master Scowler's and it was not a good life. But he might have stayed there for goodness knows how long if something had not happened to make things unbearable.

The little boots

One day, a rich gentleman asked Master Scowler to make a pair of boots for his little boy.

The boots were lovely and dazzlingly bright. Lapitch himself drove the nails into them. But when the gentleman brought his little boy to try them on, they were much too tight for him. So the gentleman didn't want to take them and he wouldn't pay for them in spite of all Master Scowler could say. When he left the shop, Master Scowler was in a fine rage and was furious with Lapitch.

'You little wretch!' he shouted. 'This is all your fault! You're a lazy good-for-nothing! It's because of you that the boots don't fit!'

When he had stopped thundering he grabbed the boots and beat Lapitch with them. He was being very unfair because he himself had cut out the boots, so it wasn't Lapitch's fault that they were so tight. But when Master Scowler was cross, his anger blinded him so that he simply couldn't tell right from wrong.

So after he had beaten Lapitch with the boots, he flung them into a corner and said to his wife: 'Burn these tomorrow. I don't want to see them any more.' Then, looking very terrifying and shaking his huge fist, he turned to Lapitch and roared: 'Even though I burn the boots, you'll still pay for them, lazybones!' And Lapitch knew that meant another beating.

So when he went to bed that night, he neither whistled nor sang but just sat thinking.

He slept in the kitchen, near the stove. He had a hard straw mattress for his bed, a ragged blanket, and a piece of candle stuck into a potato for lack of a candlestick.

He lay down and blew out the candle, which had burnt down very near the potato, and he went on thinking. After he had thought and thought for a long time, he decided that he would run away from

Master Scowler that very night to the wide world. This was not easy and not without danger but Lapitch did it. For what a shoemaker's apprentice can plan he can also carry out.

In the middle of the night, when the others were fast asleep, Lapitch got up. He felt as though he were in a box of darkness.

Noiselessly, he crept out of the kitchen and into the workshop. As he struck a match, there was a rustling, scurrying noise and the little mice, who liked to nibble the leather overnight, scattered in all directions. But Lapitch took no notice of them, for he had a lot to do to prepare for his journey.

First of all, he found a scrap of paper and a shoemaker's pencil. Then he sat down on his stool and began a letter.

'You wanted to burn the little boots,' he wrote. 'I am sorry about that so I am going away to break them in. Then they won't be too tight. Please be kinder to your new apprentice. Give him more soup and softer bread. I will return the boots to you. Lapitch.'

It took him a long time to do this as he was not very good at writing and his letters were large and scrawly.

When he had finished, he got up very quietly and pinned the note onto his master's apron which was hanging on the wall. Then he started another one. This said:

'Dear Mistress, thank you for your kindness. I am leaving but I shall not forget you and I will try to help everybody as you have helped me. Yours, Lapitch.'

Then he got up quietly again and pinned this to Mistress Scowler's apron which hung next to her husband's.

Then Lapitch took his red leather bag and crammed into it all he needed for the journey. First he put in a piece of bread and a slice of bacon. That was his supper which he had been too miserable to eat.

He added a blue handkerchief, an awl, some shoemaker's twine and several pieces of leather. Lapitch was a real shoemaker and he couldn't be without the tools of his trade any more than a soldier can be without a rifle. Then he packed his little knife and the bag was full.

Now he started to dress himself. He put on his green trousers and almost croaked out loud, he was so used to this old joke. But just in time he remembered that his master was asleep in the next room. Then he took a piece of thread and patched an elbow of his red shirt before he put it on. Lastly he put on the beautiful little boots which had earned him the beating.

He almost whistled with joy, they fitted him so well, but he swallowed the whistle because he didn't want to waken Master Scowler.

He tried on his cap but it was terribly tattered and torn. So he took a piece of shiny leather left over from the boots and made a band for it. It is rather difficult to sew leather but because he was a shoemaker he found it quite easy. Then he put the shiny cap on his head.

Now he was ready for his journey: in his green trousers, red shirt, shining little boots and bright cap, with his red leather bag slung across his back, he looked rather like a toy soldier.

Stealthily, he walked out of the workshop into the courtyard. There, the dog Bundash was chained up. He and Lapitch were great friends so Lapitch did not go near him because he knew that Bundash would whine for him. But he hated leaving him.

Just as he was wondering whether he should go and give Bundash a farewell hug, he heard his master coughing. Master Scowler was hoarse through shouting too much at his apprentice the day before and coughed in his sleep. But the sound frightened Lapitch very much. Just suppose his master wakened up! He thought he had better make haste to be off.

He ran through the front gate, which had fortunately been left unlocked, and found himself in the street. It was pitch-dark and the houses seemed to tower up to the sky. He hurried along. All was still; everybody was asleep.

That was how Lapitch ran away from Master Scowler.

The first day of the journey

The old milkman

The town was large and for a long time Lapitch walked along the streets in the dark. Soon he had gone so far that it would have been very hard for Master Scowler to find him.

But he kept on walking until it was dawn and the darkness began to melt away. In the last street of the town Lapitch met an old man who was delivering milk-cans on a cart drawn by a small donkey. The cart and the donkey were fine but the poor old man was bent and frail. He stopped his cart in front of a house that was so tall that the moon still shone upon its attic windows.

There, he lifted down a can of milk and began to take it to the door. But he tottered and stumbled on the first step and nearly fell. Sighing softly, he sat down on the steps.

Just then, he saw Lapitch in his green trousers and red shirt, his beautiful little boots and gay cap. He was so surprised that he stopped sighing.

'Let me take the milk into the house, grandfather,' said Lapitch.

'Where have you come from?' the old man asked this strange creature.

Lapitch did not want to talk about Master Scowler. So he said: 'I am an apprentice, Lapitch. The emperor has commanded me to break in these boots for his son, and to give help to everybody in his empire who might need it.'

The old man knew that Lapitch was joking, but he liked the look of him so much that he stopped his sighing and even began to chuckle.

'Where shall I take the milk?' asked Lapitch.

'Up to the third floor,' said the old man.

Lapitch was very strong, so he picked up the heavy can as though it had been a feather and carried it into the house.

The staircase was still dark. Lapitch climbed to the first floor, then to the second. When he reached the third floor, where the moon was looking in through the landing window, he saw a patch of black in the shadows and in the middle of it two specks of light, gleaming like candle flames. Of course it was a cat.

'I've brought the milk, madam,' said Lapitch. 'Please will you show me the way?'

The cat jumped up, swished her tail gently and ran in front of him, stopping at a door.

Lapitch found the bell and rang it.

A maid unlocked and opened the door.

When she saw Lapitch dressed in all his bright colours, she gave a loud scream and clapped her hands. This scared the cat, who first jumped up onto Lapitch's head, then took a leap onto the maid's shoulder and fell from there *splash* straight into a bucket of water. What a commotion! The cat squalling, the bucket rolling, the water

spilling all over the floor, Lapitch hopping nimbly away so that his boots shouldn't get wet and the maid roaring with laughter so loud that the windowpanes trembled.

'My, what a sight you are! Are you a parrot or a woodpecker?'

'Neither, miss! I'm Lapitch and I've brought your milk. The old man wasn't able to come upstairs. But you didn't have to scream.'

The maid only laughed all the louder, and took the milk from him. When Lapitch turned to go, with the empty can, she lit a candle and escorted him downstairs because he had quite taken her fancy.

'Why don't you go downstairs every day and bring up the milk?' demanded Lapitch. 'If you can come down with me now you can surely do that. The old man isn't strong and he can't carry it up all these stairs.'

The maid felt rather ashamed of herself for not thinking of this before so she promised that in future she would always go and fetch the milk.

In return, Lapitch promised that he would bring her a bunch of flowers from his journey.

When he got back to the old man he asked him whether he would let him deliver the rest of the milk. The old man was delighted to allow him to do so, so Lapitch took the donkey's reins and went on the round. The clever donkey knew all the houses where he had to stop. Lapitch was very surprised and asked the old man why such a clever animal should be called a donkey or an ass.

The milkman although very old was at a loss for an answer.

'That's what they've been called ever since *I* was born,' he said.

Lapitch was not satisfied and wished he were a better scholar.

'If I could write better I would write a book and in it I would say that these intelligent animals should have a nicer name and only creatures who deserved it should be called donkeys or asses.'

But of course the donkey didn't mind a bit about what he was called nor did he listen to the conversation. He just went on stopping at the right doors.

Every time he stopped, Lapitch would grab a can of milk and run upstairs as swiftly as the wind.

So all the milk was soon delivered. Only one small can remained, which was the old milkman's breakfast.

The old man thanked Lapitch and gave him a good drink of the lovely milk. Then he went away with his cart and Lapitch continued his journey.

Now it was broad daylight.

After a short while, Lapitch had left the town behind. Soon he could not see a single house anywhere – only vast fields, bushes, trees and the long road stretching out in front of him.

'Thank goodness!' he said to himself and sat down under a tree.

He was now missing his lost sleep. So he put his red bag under his head and stretched out in the thick grass. It was soft but not very comfortable. But Lapitch was so tired he feel asleep as easily as a rabbit in a burrow.

Sleep, Lapitch, sleep. Master Scowler is far away, and a good thing too. And better still, Lapitch doesn't know all the things that are going to happen to him – some good, some bad – on his journey. If he did know, he would not sleep so soundly.

The head in the grass

Lapitch slept long and deeply. Many carts and peasant folk passed by on the road. The carts creaked, the horses' hoofs clattered, the people shouted to one another and the geese that were being carried to market quacked and hissed.

But Lapitch might just as well have had corks in his ears for all he heard. And nobody saw him lying in the tall grass.

At noon, things quietened down and the road was empty.

Then suddenly, Lapitch was awakened. He could hear something dragging itself along in the grass, nearer and nearer towards him. Then there was a pattering sound. And then quite close, something breathed heavily and snorted. Whatever could it be?

Lapitch was sleepy but tried to sit up and see what it was. Just then, a big, shaggy, yellow head burst through the grass in front of Lapitch and stuck out a long, red tongue. It was so unexpected, it was quite frightening. Perhaps anybody else would have been alarmed but Lapitch jumped up and hugged the shaggy head.

It was his dear Bundash, who had also run away from Master Scowler and sniffed and searched and run until at last he had found Lapitch!

He started to lick Lapitch's hands and Lapitch hugged him again and again.

'Oh, good old Bundash, it's wonderful to see you!'

And the two of them rolled over and over on the grass with joy. They played till they were breathless, then Lapitch said: 'Come on, let's be quiet and have our lunch.'

But Bundash was so excited that all he wanted to do was catch flies and chase grasshoppers.

Lapitch sat on the grass and got his bread and bacon and knife out of his bag. Then he took off his cap, said his grace and began to eat. For every piece he put in his own mouth he threw one to Bundash, who

caught it in the air and swallowed it in one gulp.

In this manner Lapitch and Bundash quickly finished their lunch and then they stood up and started off again on their journey.

It was very hot and the road was long, white and dusty.

The house with the blue star

Lapitch and Bundash tramped along in very good spirits for a long time, but finally their feet began to ache.

They had just arrived at a shabby little house. It was patched and lop-sided and it had two small windows. Beneath the windows on the outside wall a big blue star was painted which could be seen for quite a way. The house looked for all the world like an old woman smiling.

Someone inside the house was weeping bitterly. Lapitch felt sorry about this and remembered what he had said about helping those in need. So he went into the house to see what was amiss.

Inside there was a boy called Marko sitting alone on a bench and crying. He was about Lapitch's size, and he was crying because he had lost a couple of geese he had been supposed to watch.

This may not seem a great misfortune, but it was to him. He had no father and his mother was poor, so Marko had been told to take great care of the geese because each was worth three hundred crowns.

When Lapitch, in his green trousers, red shirt and shiny boots, came into the room, Marko was so surprised that he stopped crying and gaped.

'What were you crying for?' asked Lapitch.

'I lost two geese I was looking after,' said Marko and started weeping even more bitterly.

'Oh, that's nothing to worry about, we'll find them. Let's go and look.'

So Lapitch, Marko and Bundash went off in quest of the geese.

Near by there was a big pond. That was where Marko always

took the geese. Lapitch had never seen so much water, as up to now he had always lived in the town. The pond was surrounded by bushes, and thick reeds grew in the water on the farther bank.

When they came to the water's edge Marko began to cry again. 'Oh, oh! I shall never find my geese.' Marko was crying so hard that Lapitch had to get his blue handkerchief out of his bag and lend it to him to wipe his tears.

He couldn't help feeling that it would be nearly impossible to find two small geese near so large a pond but he didn't want to make Marko any more miserable than he was already so he started to look among the bushes. Meanwhile Bundash was running about and sniffing and barking more and more excitedly. Suddenly he jumped into the water and started swimming across. Lapitch called, 'Bundash, Bundash,' but the dog took no notice. He only shook his head and swam on until he disappeared amongst the reeds on the other bank.

Lapitch wondered whether his dear Bundash was lost. If that happened he too would soon be crying bitterly. And he could not cry now that he had lent his handkerchief to Marko. . . . But, after all, there was no time for tears, because from across the water came the sound of the flapping of wings and loud quacking and barking. Bundash had found Marko's geese on the other side of the water where the boys could never have gone!

Marko jumped with joy when Bundash drove the geese towards him. They swam in front of the dog, opening their beaks and quacking furiously. Bundash followed, barking just as furiously.

He got the geese safely to Marko and Lapitch, then came out of the water and shook himself gaily.

'Aren't you a clever dog! When I'm rich I'll buy you a big sausage,' said Lapitch.

Then Marko took one goose and Lapitch the other, and they carried them home, whistling and singing for joy.

As they walked, Marko said: 'What a big head Bundash has!'

'That's because he has a lot of brains,' said Lapitch. 'If you had a head like that you wouldn't have needed Bundash to find your geese.'

So they got back to Marko's house. His mother had returned home and she let Lapitch sleep there because she was so pleased that his dog had found the geese. So Bundash had secured for Lapitch his first night's lodgings.

By now it was evening so Marko and Lapitch sat down on a big stone in front of the house and got polenta with milk in a coloured bowl and two big, wooden spoons.

While they were eating, Lapitch asked Marko: 'Who drew the blue star on the house?'

'I did,' said Marko. 'When Mother painted the room I took some paint and drew the star. I thought the geese would remember it and know where their home was. But now I know that I was wrong and that geese swim across the water, star or no star.'

But Lapitch remembered the blue star very well (and everybody reading this book should remember it too). He little knew then how helpful it would be to him when he got into serious danger....

So the two boys talked and ate and Bundash got some polenta too. And afterwards they all went to bed.

Of course Lapitch did not sleep in the house or in a bed because there was no room for him.

In the yard there was a small cowshed and he slept in the loft over this.

He had to climb up a ladder and creep in through a small hole. When he had got up there, he turned and poked his head through the hole and called out: 'Good night.'

The yard was deserted. The night was very dark and the yard looked like a great black hollow but there were more stars in the sky than Lapitch had ever seen before. He took off his beautiful boots, wiped them, lay down on the hay and fell fast asleep.

Bundash slept in front of the cowshed, Lapitch slept over it and inside it slept a beautiful spotted cow.

This was the first day of Lapitch's travels, and it had a happy ending. What would the next day bring?

The second day of the journey

Lapitch and the stone-breakers

Early next morning, the cocks started crowing, the geese started quacking, the cow jangled its bell and Bundash barked and whined because he could not see Lapitch.

There was such a lot of noise that Lapitch woke up, and at first thought he must be in a menagerie. In a village there is always this kind of noise in the morning, but he did not yet know that.

So Lapitch sat up, put on his boots and went down the ladder. He thanked Marko's mother and she gave him a big piece of bread and three boiled eggs to eat on his way.

Lapitch and Bundash set out again. It was the only quiet morning they had on their journey.

For some time they walked on feeling cheerful and carefree. Then they came to a part of the road where men were sitting beating stones with long hammers. Some of them wore big black goggles because they were afraid of getting dust or chips of stone in their eyes. Others had no goggles and were not afraid but sang merrily as they worked.

Lapitch liked these men better and so he sat down and joined them in their song.

After they had sung for some time, Lapitch asked the stone-breakers whether the life of a traveller was hard. The stone-breakers naturally knew how to answer this question as in their work on the road they always saw the travellers who passed.

One of the workmen said: 'A man who has good boots, strong hands and a clever head doesn't find travelling difficult.'

'And what about the people who don't have these things?'

'Well, they don't find any difficulties either because when they get to the first village they're sick of the journey and go home.'

Lapitch stood up to go. But before he went they had a good laugh together over something funny that happened.

A very small, spotted calf appeared from somewhere. It didn't seem to know where it was going – little calves never do – but it wanted a fight with Lapitch. It lowered its spotted head, and rushed at him.

The stone-breakers burst out laughing.

'May the best one win! You're just of a size!'

Lapitch laughed.

'We may be the same size but I don't think we're properly matched.'

Slap! slap! Then, thump! thump! Lapitch beat the calf with his hard little hands and the calf butted him with its spotted head.

Then the calf backed away and came at him again.

'Come on, charge away!' shouted Lapitch.

And charge it did!

Lapitch dodged nimbly aside. The calf dashed past him and tumbled like a pumpkin into the ditch.

Lapitch clapped his hands on his knees and laughed and laughed to see the calf thrashing about in the ditch. When it staggered to its feet again it lifted its spotted tail, suddenly remembered where its mother was and fled towards her. Lapitch dusted himself down and said: 'I once read a verse in the shoemaker's calendar. It went:

When fools and wise men have a fight,
The wise will find the struggle light.'

Then he said goodbye to the stone-breakers and they wished him a pleasant journey, adding: 'Your boots are good and you've just proved you have strong hands and a clever head.'

Lapitch set off on his journey again, pleased by what they had said.

It was a hot, sultry day and a storm was brewing. There would be sure to be some thunder, lightning and rain by the evening.

The man in black

Towards evening, Lapitch was still walking. He had passed through a village but decided not to stop there. He wanted to get as far away as possible from Master Scowler. So he tramped on and on until eventually a strong wind began to blow, lightning flashed and thunder rumbled, at first in the distance and then nearer and nearer.

It sounded just as though somebody were driving a heavy iron wagon across the sky. Bundash was terrified of thunder and kept close to his master.

'This is nothing to make a fuss about,' said Lapitch and kept on walking. Then there came a huge flash of lightning and a thunderbolt crashed in the distance. Bundash trembled with fear but Lapitch said: 'And *that*'s nothing to make a fuss about either. Come on.'

A strong wind got up. He had to hold onto his cap so that it shouldn't be blown away. Then the clouds went so black it was as dark as night, except when the lightning came, and it looked as if the whole sky had caught fire. Then the rain started in a heavy downpour.

'Now we'd better find shelter,' said Lapitch, feeling worried most about his boots. He looked about him but there were no houses or people, only fields and trees. There didn't seem anywhere to go.

It was a good thing that Lapitch and Bundash were together. They made good partners, because sometimes one was more clever and sometimes the other and so they always helped each other.

This time Bundash was the clever one. A little farther along the road, he saw a bridge and barked to draw Lapitch's attention to it.

'Good old Bundash. Aren't you bright!' said Lapitch, and they got underneath the bridge.

But as he crawled under the bridge Lapitch shrank back. Who would not have been afraid! A man in a long black overcoat and battered hat was sitting under there. Bundash started barking furiously at him, but this time Lapitch was the cleverer for he knew that one should always be kind and polite. So he told Bundash to be quiet and said to the man: 'Good evening.'

'Good evening,' replied the man, 'How did *you* get here?'

'It's raining very heavily outside and I don't want to get my boots wet,' said Lapitch, 'May Bundash and I take shelter here?'

'You can if you like, but it's not a very nice place.'

It certainly wasn't very nice under the bridge. They couldn't stand up but only sit or crouch.

The wind blew harder still, the rain and hail pattered on the bridge above them like showers of bullets and the thunder was so loud that they could not hear each other speak.

So the three of them crouched under the bridge and all the time Bundash was growling at the man. Lapitch did not like him either. He would have felt much happier if he and Bundash had been by themselves.

By nightfall, the storm was still raging.

'We'll have to sleep here,' said the man.

Lapitch saw that he was right. The rain was pouring down in torrents so it was impossible for them to go on.

Under the bridge there was a heap of straw as though somebody had slept there before.

Lapitch spread it out so that he and the man could share it.

Then he took off his boots, wiped them carefully and put them by his side. He put his bag under his head and lay down.

The man pulled his overcoat around him and lay down too. Lapitch said, 'Good night,' the man answered, 'Good night,' then Lapitch began to say his prayers out loud. The man didn't pray. He only turned away and began to snore like a wolf.

Lapitch felt uneasy. He hugged Bundash for warmth and comfort.

This was the second day of their journey. It had not been too good but every journey has its troubles. Anyway, Lapitch could look forward to putting his boots on again in the morning. That was a pleasing thought to go to sleep on and soon he slept.

The third day of the journey

A sad blow

During the night, Bundash suddenly snarled and barked. Lapitch, who was very tired, hugged him tighter still and told him to be quiet. So Bundash stopped making a noise and they slept on.

When it was daylight Lapitch awoke and saw at once that the man in the black overcoat had gone. He was not sorry, in fact he felt relieved, so he got up cheerfully and reached for his boots.

What a shock! This was terrible.

The boots had disappeared. Lapitch hunted in and under the hay but they were nowhere to be found. The man had taken them.

'Oh, my beautiful boots!' sighed Lapitch, when he saw what had happened. Gravely he clasped his hands and sat there thinking.

Any child would cry if someone stole his beautiful boots, especially if he had to go barefoot on a long journey. But Lapitch did not. He just thought for a while, then he called Bundash.

'We'll look for him, Bundash, and we'll find him if it takes us ten years! And we'll get the boots back, even if he hides them in the emperor's chimney!'

So, barefoot, Lapitch set out to look for his boots, and that was no easy task. The world is very big and there are many places in it where the man in black could have hidden them.

This was the beginning of his strangest adventures.

Gita

Lapitch walked and walked along the road trying to puzzle out a way of finding his boots. It was very difficult indeed.

After he had been walking for about half an hour, he saw a beautiful little girl walking ahead of him.

She had long hair and a small green parrot sat on her shoulder. She was walking quickly and carrying her clothes in a bundle tied up in a red handkerchief.

Her name was Gita. She belonged to a circus,

Lapitch liked the look of her very much for she was wearing a blue dress trimmed with silver ribbons. The dress was fairly shabby, it is true, but what did that matter? She wore white shoes with golden buckles and they were old and patched too, but that did not seem to matter either. Lapitch made haste to catch up with her.

'Good morning,' he said, when he did so. But what a surprise when the parrot answered for her!

'Good morning, good morning, good morning,' it said. It was such a chatterbox that it would have gone on saying good morning for a week and a day if Gita had not held its beak.

Gita and Lapitch began to talk.

She told him how her master had left her behind in a village when she was ill. He had gone a long way ahead past two villages and one town and had told her to catch him up when she was well again.

'I've been through two villages already,' she said; 'it seems a very long journey.'

'I'm on a journey, too,' said Lapitch, 'so let's go together.'

'All right,' said Gita. 'I'm feeling very sad,' she went on. 'This morning, while I went to get a drink from a well, I left my box by the roadside. When I came back it was gone. Someone had stolen it. There were all sorts of things in it including my gold earrings.'

'Somebody stole my boots, too,' said Lapitch. 'Don't worry. We'll find the earrings and the boots, you'll see. Come on.'

'But I'm very hungry,' said Gita.

'Oh, dear,' thought Lapitch, 'first she is miserable and now she's hungry. I suppose all girls are a bit difficult.'

But he thought her very beautiful and tried to comfort her.

'We are sure to find some work in the next village and then we won't be hungry any more. We must offer to work for some farmer. What can you do?'

Gita tossed her head proudly.

'Everything! I can ride and I can stand up on a horse and make it jump through a hoop. I can juggle with twelve apples at a time, I can bite through a thick glass tumbler and swallow the pieces and I know plenty more things that people do in a circus.'

Lapitch burst out laughing so heartily that his cap fell off.

'I don't think the things you can do will be much use to us. If you juggle with apples and swallow glass tumblers I don't think any farmer will hire you.'

Gita was offended. But then Lapitch gave her his last piece of bread and they agreed they would look for work together. So they made for the next village.

Lapitch walked on one side, Gita on the other and Bundash in the middle. Gita's parrot perched on her shoulder. They marched like soldiers to a tune that Lapitch whistled, so it seemed no time at all before they reached the village.

Haymaking

Lapitch saw a farmer mowing hay amongst his labourers. He went up to him and said: 'Could you use good workers?'

The farmer was amused because Lapitch and Gita were so small and were dressed in such bright colours, and because of their parrot and dog.

'Why do you think *you* are good workers?' he asked.

'Because we don't know anything but we'd like to learn all we can,' said Lapitch.

This answer pleased the farmer and, although he had never had workers that looked like Lapitch and Gita, he told them they could help to turn over the hay: he wanted it to dry as soon as possible.

The farm labourers were still eating their breakfast so they shared their bread and bacon with the two children.

When they had all finished eating, they started work. Gita put her bundle and parrot on the branch of a tree.

The children were each given a huge pitchfork, and they were supposed to turn the hay over and then pile it into heaps.

Lapitch was very strong and skilful and the hay fairly flew round him as he worked.

But Gita was lazy. She had never learnt any work like this in the circus and she soon became bored.

She only turned over a bit of hay and then piled it into an untidy heap and sat down on it.

'Lapitch, I'm hot.'

Lapitch did not answer and went on with his work.

'Lapitch, I'm hungry again,' said Gita after a while.

Still Lapitch took no notice. He piled up the hay neatly and had soon made three high stacks. Gita became very angry because he did not answer her, and hated the work still more.

First she jabbed her pitchfork around clumsily and broke it. Then, crosser than ever, she began to rake the grass and did it so badly that the rake lost three of its teeth. Finally she began to mix dry grass with fresh. The farmer saw her and decided he did not need her. No work, no bread!

So with a stick in his hand he went towards Gita to drive her away. This is what farmers do to lazy workers. After all, grass has to be mown. . . . If they didn't do that they might as well not start haymaking at all.

But Gita saw him coming with the stick so she got away quickly before he could get too near. She threw away her rake, picked up her parrot and bundle and disappeared into the bushes as lithe as a squirrel.

Bundash, who also preferred play to work, bounded after her. Behind the bushes was a small cart for carrying drinking-water. There Gita and Bundash hid themselves.

'And don't let me see you here again!' shouted the farmer.

So Gita had lost her job. But who knows what was brewing in her little circus-performer's head?

Lapitch saw everything that happened, and he was disappointed. But he went on working and thought to himself, 'It isn't Gita's fault, she hasn't been taught this kind of work. Since we're travelling together I shall have to look after her, so I will give her half my dinner.'

So Lapitch worked away cheerfully all day to earn enough dinner for the two of them.

Gita, Bundash and the parrot did not appear until it was quite late. They had probably lunched on wild berries in the bushes. No one knew what they were up to all day – until the evening.

It was a happy evening so it is worth telling it in full, although it is not otherwise important. For most people the cheerful things are the most important, anyway.

The performance

In the evening, when their work was over, all the labourers sat down to eat. There were so many of them that the table was nearly twenty feet long. It was set underneath a big oak tree, and the farmer's wife brought out four big dishes of beans and three still larger ones of potatoes. Lapitch sat down to eat with them.

He was just wondering how he could find Gita and give her some food, when suddenly, a trumpet sounded from amongst the bushes.

Everybody looked up and they were so startled that they all dropped their spoons. For what they saw coming along the path was a breath-taking sight.

Gita, dressed in a golden gown, was riding in the little cart that had held the drinking-water. It was decorated with flowers and Bundash was pulling it. He had a wreath of flowers round his neck and red bows on his tail, and flowers were even twisted round the reins. A pole was tied to the front of the cart and from a ring attached to this swung the parrot.

But Gita was the most dazzling sight. She sat there like a queen in her golden dress, her hair streaming over her shoulders. She was blowing a small golden trumpet. This and the dress and the ribbons she had, of course, taken from her bundle.

Bundash dragged the cart towards the labourers.

How the clever dog had been trained to do this in such a short time was Gita's secret. How wonderful for Lapitch to share his journey with a friend who was wise and good in joy and in need!

All the men burst out laughing and rejoicing: they were full of admiration for Gita and Bundash.

Then Gita jumped down from the cart and the show began. She spread out a tarpaulin to make a stage and began to dance. She spun like a top and hopped like a bird and beat a little drum.

Every now and again she would jump through a hoop she held in her hand. The hoop was very small but she passed through it as easily as a fairy.

All this was very exciting, but something still better was in store.

Gita produced a rope and tied the ends to two oak trees. Then, climbing up as easily as a cat, she spread out her arms and started to walk on the thin rope high above the ground.

Lapitch was terrified and ran to the rope ready to catch her if she fell. But Gita only laughed and walked as easily on her tightrope as anybody else would on the ground. When she got to the end she jumped down lightly.

'Oh, oh, I've never seen anything like that before!' said Lapitch, and he thought to himself gleefully that it would be much easier than he had supposed to find Gita's earrings and his boots. For if the man in black had hidden them in a cellar, Gita, who had jumped through that small hoop so easily, would surely be able to crawl in, even perhaps through a mousehole: if he had hidden them in a loft, Gita, so used to heights, would be able to prowl over the rooftops and look into all the lofts and attics. She would be certain to find her box and the boots.

But of course Lapitch was wrong: Gita had been trained for hoops and tightropes just for the sake of hoops and tightropes. This didn't mean that she would be good at getting into cellars and attics.

Meanwhile, all the labourers were so full of admiration for Gita's skill that they were forgetting to eat their beans and potatoes.

Then Gita went to the cart again, picked up the pole with the parrot in the ring and lifted it high above her head. Then she started to beat the drum slowly with her foot, and to sing a strange kind of song which only circus people and parrots understand.

The parrot began to turn round and round on its ring. It hung upside down, holding on by its claws, it held on by its beak and let its claws swing and then it started bowing and putting its head on one side like a Chinese lady. It did a sort of bear's dance, then whistled like a steam engine and started to turn somersaults so fast that it looked like nothing but a blur of colours.

For her final surprise Gita raised the pole, shouted 'Good night' and waved the pole towards Lapitch. Immediately the parrot flew off it and perched on Lapitch's shoulder, it took off his cap and threw it on the ground, shouting 'Good night, good night, good night' over and over again. Gita was screaming with laughter and so was the parrot.

Everybody, even the farmer, laughed at that. Only Lapitch was so astonished that he stood there speechless, with the parrot on his shoulder.

'Good night, good night, good night,' chorused the labourers, echoing the parrot, and finally Lapitch joined in the merriment. He took the parrot from his shoulder, put it on the ground and covered it with his cap.

'Now make a bow if you can!' he said.

But of course the parrot couldn't do it, for a boy's cap covers the wisest parrot from head to tail.

The parrot and the cap simply ran round and round blindly until Gita picked up the cap and freed it.

That was the end of the entertainment and Gita was given some beans and potatoes. The farmer wasn't cross with her any more because he hadn't been able to help laughing, and you can't be cross if you are laughing.

'Didn't I do well? Didn't you like my work?' Gita demanded.

'Work like that is all very well,' Lapitch told her, '– when there is nothing else to do.'

Conversation in the hay

That night, the farmer's wife took Gita to sleep in the house. Lapitch slept outside on the hay with all the labourers. When he had settled down, he sighed deeply and said: 'I didn't find my boots today.'

'What boots?' asked a labourer who was lying next to him.

'Somebody stole them, early this morning.'

'That's funny. Somebody stole my blue coat.'

'Somebody stole my axe,' said another man.

'Somebody stole a ham from my loft,' said another.

'And I lost a bag of money....'

So they all knew that there was a thief in the village and started wondering who he could be and trying to think of ways of getting their property back.

Then the moon rose in the sky and one by one they dropped off to sleep.

The fourth day of the journey

Fire, fire!

Never in his life had Lapitch slept as well as he did that night. It is lovely to sleep on hay in the summer. The hay smells wonderful, everything is peaceful, nobody is awake. In the country all good people sleep at night. Only owls and bats are about and even they fly silently. They could not wake up Lapitch.

Alas, when everything seems perfect something usually happens to spoil it.

Lapitch was roused by the labourers shouting, 'Fire, fire!'

He quickly jumped up. It was still dark but in the village there was a bright light as red as a furnace coming from a huge fire blazing there. A stable belonging to a farmer known as 'Bad Gregory' was burning. Nobody in the village liked Gregory. But when somebody's place is burning, likes and dislikes are forgotten. Everybody must help to put out the fire.

So all the men ran towards the village to help and Lapitch ran to join them.

Men were coming out of their houses, carrying long poles with hooks to help beat out the fire. Women were running with water buckets, and crying children were running clinging to their mothers' aprons. There was a terrific lot of noise and shouting as they ran towards the blazing stable.

Because this was a small village there was no fire brigade and Lapitch wondered whatever they would do without one.

But the people were very clever and didn't need a fire brigade at all. They formed themselves into a long line, so long that the man at one end of the line was next to the fire, the one at the other was next to the well. The one at the well filled a pail with water and passed it to the man next to him and so it went swiftly all down the line until it reached the last man. He was perched on a ladder and hurled the water onto the burning stable. He was so strong that he threw the water as high as a fireman's hose.

This chain system worked very well and yet everybody shouted: 'Hurry up! Hurry up!' They passed the pails of water as quickly as they could because they didn't want the fire to spread from the stable to the house.

But it was no use. When the stable fire was put out, they saw the house had caught alight because its roof was made of wooden shingles.

How dreadful it is when a house catches fire! All the women and children screamed when the roof began to crack. And because their exertions had made them very tired the men began to quarrel.

'Somebody must go onto the roof and squirt water from there,' one man shouted.

'*I* shan't go up there, I'd fall into the fire,' snapped another.

'You're all cowards!' jeered a third.

They wrangled so much that the house would certainly have burned down and perhaps even the caps on their heads would have caught fire before they felt like stopping. But just then somebody called from the roof:

'Pass me up a bucket of water, quickly!'

Everybody looked up and there sat a little figure, wearing green trousers, a red shirt and a coloured cap. Some of you would have thought it was a fireman. But of course it was Lapitch who had scrambled up there while the people were wasting time quarrelling.

The men quickly began to hoist up one bucket of water after another on the ends of their hooked poles. Lapitch sat astride the ridge of the roof, pouring the water onto the blaze, but it came nearer and nearer him. The flames were flaring and burning more and more fiercely. The women wailed: 'Oh, the child will be burnt to death on that roof!'

The flames had almost reached Lapitch's feet and he was very hot and tired because he had lifted so many heavy buckets. His hands began to tremble. Below him, all the villagers trembled too because they were so afraid of what might happen to him.

By this time, Lapitch had realized that he could not manage to put out the fire with the buckets of water, and the heat was so great that he could hardly breathe.

'Give me a pole,' he shouted hoarsely.

They passed him a pole with an iron hook.

As hard as he could he beat the burning shingles beneath him.

Sparks flew around him like stars, flames hissed at him like snakes. Then a crackling and splintering was heard. The burning shingles crashed through the flames and the entire burning corner of the roof collapsed and fell onto the ground. Now the villagers were able to rush up and beat out the fire. The house was saved!

But alas, Lapitch had disappeared. The ridge on which he had been sitting broke and he fell into the loft.

Poor Lapitch! He was good, so willing to help! And now nobody knew whether he was alive or dead!

The miracle

What happened to Lapitch when he fell into the loft really was a miracle. He must have been very good to deserve not only a wonderful escape but another stroke of luck, too – as you will hear.

First then, when he fell into the loft he fell – oh, wonder of wonders – straight into a bin of flour. It was as soft as feathers and Lapitch was quite unhurt.

But you would never guess what Lapitch saw when he looked about him.

His own beautiful boots were hanging in the loft right before his eyes.

A little farther away, there hung the first man's coat, next to it the second man's axe and then the third man's ham; and right in the corner the box with the money belonging to the fourth man. On the floor was Gita's little white box.

'Hurrah, hurrah!' yelled Lapitch, sitting in the flour like a mouse in a bran-tub. 'Hurrah, come up everybody! I caught my boots flying through the air!'

The people thought that Lapitch's fall had knocked him silly. You don't catch boots in the air like butterflies. But all the same they ran upstairs.

And there they saw all the things they had lost. The attic looked like a pawnbroker's shop! Now they knew why Gregory prowled about at night. They knew that Gregory and the man in the black coat were working together and that they hid what they stole in Gregory's attic.

Everybody rejoiced and reclaimed what he had lost, but the most delighted of all was the man who found his bag with the money.

They picked Lapitch out of the flour and carried him shoulder-high to the courtyard. Nursing his precious boots, he felt as happy as a king.

Gregory's mother

Everybody felt happy except Gregory's old, sick mother who lay in her bed weeping. Until that night, she had not known what a wicked son she had. He was not at home, he was out on the prowl, but she was afraid that if the villagers found him they would give him a good beating. She could hear them talking down in the courtyard.

‘If Gregory were here we’d beat him up,’ said one man.

‘I’d like to bash his head,’ said another.

‘Or throw him into the fire,’ suggested a third.

And so they went on.

That wouldn’t get them anywhere, thought Lapitch. Beating up Gregory wouldn’t make him any better. So he went up to Gregory’s mother’s room and whispered to her: ‘Don’t cry. I know Gregory because yesterday some of the men pointed him out to me when he went across the field. When I go on my way tomorrow, if I meet him I’ll warn him about returning to the village. I’ll tell him to stop being friends with the man in black and go away and lead an honest life.’

‘God bless you, my child,’ said the poor old woman, and she immediately felt happier. She saw that there was one person at least who meant her son no harm.

Then Gregory’s mother gave Lapitch a handkerchief with a silver coin tied up in it.

‘Give this to my poor Gregory, if you meet him,’ she begged, and burst into tears again.

Lapitch promised that he would, took the handkerchief, said good-bye and went out into the courtyard.

It was empty because the people had all gone home, rejoicing over the property they had recovered. Then Lapitch picked up Gita’s box and took it back to her. She was delighted and hugged Lapitch so hard that Bundash started barking, because he thought she meant to strangle him.

By now it was broad daylight and nobody wanted to go back to bed.

The scar

Next day was an uneventful one and a good thing too because everybody was so tired. Nobody in the village did much work that day but they talked a great deal. At every garden fence there were a couple of women gossiping about the fire, under every tree three or four men lay talking about the fire, and in all the ditches were children playing. But the children were catching frogs – the fire already forgotten.

Everybody said Lapitch was a hero. He had a burnt heel, since he had done his firefighting barefoot. When Gita bandaged it for him, he said: 'You know, I'm glad that man took my boots.'

'Gracious, why?' asked Gita.

'Because if I had had them on when I was putting out the fire, *their* heels might have been burnt. That would have been a pity. But my heel will soon be better.'

Gita was much impressed because he didn't make a fuss and thought how much she would have cried if *she* had had a burn. Wanting to show off, she stuck out her right thumb.

'I had a wound once,' she said, and sure enough there was a scar on her thumb, shaped like a cross.

'Where did you get that?' asked Lapitch, 'Did it hurt much?'

'I don't remember when I got it. It was when I was quite small before I joined the circus.'

'Where were you before you joined the circus?'

'I don't remember that either.'

'But who took you there?'

'I don't know. My master says I haven't any parents and I wish I hadn't got him either because I don't like him. He's got very cruel-looking eyes. And once, in the night, I heard him plotting with some people. I'm sure he's a very wicked man.' She thought for a while, then added: 'Most of all I wish I had a mother. What is it like to have a mother, Lapitch?'

'I don't know,' said Lapitch, 'because I haven't got one either. But my master's wife was very kind and often protected me from him. When I was very tired in the evenings she used to take the broom out of my hands and do my sweeping for me. I expect having a mother means you have someone who will always be kind to you.'

'Then I wish your master's wife could be my mother,' said Gita.

Lapitch wanted to explain that this was impossible but before he could get very far the villagers called him. They were barbecuing a lamb in his honour and he had to go to help and turn the spit.

That evening everybody was very merry. They feasted on roast meat and cake, and the farmer and his wife asked Lapitch to stay another night so that his foot would be better.

The fifth day of the journey

In the meadows

The next day Lapitch and Gita didn't like saying goodbye to the villagers. They felt as though they had known them for years. This was because they had been through the fire. Great danger draws people closer together.

When they saw that Lapitch and Gita were sorry to go, the villagers stuffed their bags full of food, meat and bread and cakes, because that was the only way they could think of to comfort them. In the end Lapitch's bag looked like a big, fat bumble-bee.

Gita couldn't help laughing at it, so they parted from their friends gaily.

Their road lay amongst vast meadows, like a long piece of straw laid across a green sea, and Lapitch and Gita walked along the road like two ants along the straw.

After they had walked a long distance, they came to a place where the road branched off in two directions. One went farther across the vast plain and the other went up a mountain and into a forest. This was the crossroads.

In the olden days, people used to tell stories about elves and witches and vampires meeting at crossroads. But these days there are no such creatures. Possibly, in summer, you might see a young shepherd whittling sticks or eating berries, or in winter, hares playing in the snow under a full moon.

Today, in a meadow near the crossroads, Lapitch and Gita saw a number of herdboys and girls, looking after their cows and roasting corn on the cob over a fire.

There were five little herders, two girls and three boys. The youngest was so small that the tall grasses tickled his nose. He walked about dressed only in a shirt that was too long for him. He was a chubby little boy called Mishko.

All the cowherds crowded round Gita and Lapitch and Bundash and the parrot and wondered at them. They asked them all kinds of questions and little Mishko thought that Lapitch was a soldier in uniform. He pointed his finger at him and said: 'When you grow up, soldier, your cap will be too small for you.'

Lapitch didn't much like people to talk about his being small. So he retorted: 'And when *you* grow up, you'll be able to wear the same shirt. It will be just right for you.'

'Don't be rude to Mishko,' snapped Mishko's elder brother.

'I wasn't being rude, I was only joking,' protested Lapitch.

Then the brother squared up to Lapitch, looked him up and down and said: 'I don't call that much of a joke. You'd better stop talking that way to my brother.'

Lapitch had been an apprentice long enough to know that when boys talked like that they usually want to fight.

But although he was stronger than any of the cowherds, he didn't want to start scrapping.

So he said to Mishko's brother:

'Don't let's fight, let's see who can throw a stone the farthest. Then we'll know which of us is the stronger.'

Lapitch picked up a big piece of rock and hoisted it on his shoulder as though it were as light as a feather. Then from that position he tossed it with the full thrust of his arm. It flew over the trees and bushes and far away into the meadow.

Robin Hood as a boy might have matched that throw, but not one of the herdboys could. Mishko's brother was silent; he was glad he hadn't had a fight with Lapitch. And the girls, who didn't like fighting anyway, said to one another: 'That boy is stronger and wiser than Mishko's brother.'

Meanwhile, the other children had taken Gita to the fire where the corn was roasting.

'Listen to it crackling!' she exclaimed. 'Oh, do let's stay here for a little while.'

Lapitch didn't mind because he knew the herders admired him and he was pleased about it. And it was very pleasant in the meadow.

Herders have a lovely time when they sit round a fire roasting corn or potatoes. No words can describe it. Anyway, it's better not to try, for everybody can't be as happy as herders and it might only make less fortunate people sorry reading about them.

Well, Gita and Lapitch had come, so more corn had to be gathered because there were two more mouths to be fed.

'But are you allowed to take the corn?' asked Lapitch.

'We are because we guard it,' explained the herders.

'But if you take it, how can you say you guard it?'

'We guard it from the cows. If we weren't here there wouldn't be any corn at all,' said one of the herdboys, proudly. And they went to gather some more for their guests. Only Mishko stayed behind to look after the fire.

Before they went for the corn, Lapitch took off his boots because the grass was wet and he wanted to keep them dry.

He saw little Mishko looking at them and said: 'Don't touch these boots, Mishko. They belong to a king and if you put them on they'll bite you.'

'They certainly will,' said one of the herdboys, and slipped some nettles into the boots when Mishko wasn't looking.

When Mishko was left alone, he stared at the boots for a long time and the more he looked at them the more beautiful they seemed. In the end he simply couldn't believe that they would bite him.

So he sidled up to them and put his hand inside one of them and of course got stung by the nettles.

'Ow-ww!' he wailed. 'They really do bite!'

And then something dawned on him. The little boy had often been stung by nettles and knew how it felt, so he guessed what it was in the boots. He wrapped his hand in his long shirt and took the nettles out of the boots.

When Lapitch and Gita and the others came back, Mishko met them wearing Lapitch's boots. They nearly came up to his waist and he looked so funny that Lapitch simply couldn't be angry with him.

'Well, Mishko, didn't they bite you?' asked Lapitch.

'Yes, they did, but I've pulled their teeth out.'

This made everybody laugh. Then Mishko took off the boots and gave them back to Lapitch, who put them on again and both of them were happy. If everyone were as kind as Lapitch, two people could be happy with only one pair of boots.

Then they all sat round the fire. The girls fanned it with their aprons and the boys stuck the corncobs on long sticks to roast them. Lapitch told them all about Master Scowler, the man in black and the wicked Gregory.

'Now the most important thing I must do is to find him and give him the handkerchief and the silver coin his mother entrusted to me,' said Lapitch.

'How will you find him?' asked Gita.

'I don't know. But I do so want to give it to him, and I'm wishing so hard that I think he might drop from the skies at my feet.'

'You may be sure he won't,' said the oldest herdboy, laughing. 'Even fruit doesn't drop from the skies unless you sit under the tree, so why should a man?'

A man drops from the skies

Hardly had the herdboy made this remark when there was a terrific noise on the road that led down from the mountains: sounds of rolling wheels and galloping hooves, yells and curses.

Everybody sprang up to look.

A cart drawn by two horses was clattering along at great speed. Something had frightened the horses and made them bolt.

They were tossing their heads and foaming with fear. The cart was tipping and rolling from side to side.

It looked as though it would topple into the ditch at any minute.

Two terrified men sat in it. One of them was pulling at a rein: the other rein, broken and flying loose, kept flicking the horses and increasing their panic so that they galloped faster than ever, quite out of control.

'Come on,' shouted Lapitch, 'we must stop the horses.'

He ran into the road and stood in the middle of it, waving his hands and shouting. He had seen bolting horses pulled up in this way before.

The cart was still some distance away but it was frightening to watch it hurtling straight at him.

But just before it got right up to Lapitch, the cart swerved, a wheel hit the rocks by the road and the cart turned over with a terrible crash. The horses reared up, their hooves flailing, and the men were catapulted into the ditch.

'Whoa!' yelled Lapitch. And 'Whoa!' cried Gita and all the little herders who had followed Lapitch. And the horses, snorting like fiery dragons, pulled up. Gita ran to them and grabbed their reins in her little hands.

'Oh,' she cried, 'look how beautiful this one is! Let's take him out of the shafts, I want to have a ride on him. He's nearly as beautiful as my Soko!'

She remembered her horse at the circus and she was so excited and happy that she couldn't think of anything else.

But Lapitch knew that there were more important things to do. He left Gita and the herders to see to the horses and went over to the ditch to see what had happened to the two men. He didn't know what a surprise he was going to have: of course, if he had, it wouldn't have been a surprise! In the ditch were lying – oh Lord! Lapitch's blood ran cold – in the ditch were lying the man in black and Gregory. They were just trying to scramble out when Lapitch arrived.

Lapitch didn't know quite what to do, so he said what you can always say: 'Good afternoon!'

'A very good afternoon, I must say, when your cart goes into a ditch!' growled the man in black in a voice that seemed to come from the grave.

'It *is* a good afternoon because you didn't kill yourselves,' said

Lapitch. And he thought that it was also a good afternoon because he could now give Gregory his handkerchief and silver coin. But what will happen when the man in black sees that I have found my boots? thought Lapitch.

But the man was in such a hurry that he hardly noticed Lapitch. As soon as he got out of the ditch, he yelled at Gregory:

'What are you dawdling for? We're sound in wind and limb and we've no time to waste. Come on, let's go and look to the horses!'

So Gregory got out of the ditch and they went to the horses. But Bundash recognized the man in black and set on him, tugging at his overcoat. The man kicked him and snarled: 'I've heard your barking before.'

And then his eye fell upon Lapitch and he remembered him – and his boots!

For a moment he stood motionless. He didn't say anything but his face showed all kinds of terrible thoughts.

He looked at Lapitch as a snake looks at a rabbit.

But Lapitch, though he was small, stood bolt upright and looked the man in black straight in the eye and thought: Whatever happens you'll never get my boots again!

And Bundash growled and showed his teeth and dared the man to lay hands on Lapitch.

It looked terrifying.... But then the man in black muttered: 'We must go – we're in a hurry.' And he yelled to Gregory: 'Harness the horses, fool!'

'The reins are broken,' complained Gregory. 'It's no use, we can't go on.'

'But we *must* go on!' shouted the man in black and snatched up the reins to see what was the matter with them.

Then something quite unexpected happened. Lapitch went up to him and said: 'I will mend the reins.'

'What do you mean, Puss-in-Boots, *you*'ll mend the reins?' The man gave Lapitch a contemptuous glance.

'I *am* wearing boots, although I had to go without them for two days,' retorted Lapitch, 'but I am no *Puss*-in-Boots. If I were a cat I wouldn't know how to mend reins, but as it is I am Lapitch, a shoemaker's apprentice, I have some good strong twine in my bag and I'll do the job for you because you seem to be in a hurry.'

Very few would mend reins for a man who had stolen their boots! But Lapitch took an awl and some twine and some leather out of his bag and went over to the horses to get the harness.

When the man in black saw that Lapitch really meant what he said, he muttered: 'Well, you're a good boy. Mend the reins quickly and we'll forget about the boots.'

'Certainly,' said Lapitch, 'I'd rather wear them than think about them.'

And he sat down on a heap of stones and began to mend the reins. As soon as he started sewing he began to sing and whistle just as he used to in Master Scowler's workshop.

He nearly forgot what he had to tell Gregory, who sat down to help him while the man in black went off to try to repair the cart.

Meanwhile, Gita and the herders led the horses into the meadow.

Gregory and Lapitch

When Lapitch was left alone with Gregory, he said to him: 'Gregory, I'll make a good job of mending the reins and then you had better drive far away. Don't go back to your own village whatever you do because the people are waiting to kill you.'

Gregory said nothing and stared at Lapitch's boots. He now realized that the farmers knew that he and the man in black were thieves.

Lapitch tried again. 'Gregory, your mother has given me something for you but I won't give it to you until you promise what I ask.'

'What do you want me to promise?' muttered Gregory.

'To leave the man in black, go far away and find somewhere where you can learn an honest living. Your sick mother has sent you this message and she was crying when she gave me this for you.'

Lapitch took the handkerchief and silver coin out of his bag and handed it to Gregory.

When Gregory saw his mother's handkerchief and gift and heard her message, his heart softened and he felt as though he had become a child again. This sometimes happens to grown-up people when they remember their mothers.

But Gregory didn't have much time to talk to Lapitch because the man in black was returning. Gregory stuffed the handkerchief into his pocket and whispered: 'Mend the reins well, and God bless you, my boy.'

At that moment the man in black joined them.

'The reins are ready,' said Lapitch, who had just finished the job.

'Bring those horses at once,' shouted the man in black.

Gita and the herders led them up. One of them was black and glossy with a long mane and long tail.

'I don't suppose I'll ever see him again,' sighed Gita as he was harnessed.

'I should think not, you grasshopper,' snapped the man in black. 'Where he goes *you* aren't likely to go! Come on, less talking, we must be off!'

He jumped onto the cart and Gregory sat down by him, looking miserable.

That's a good sign, thought Lapitch. If he has the grace to look miserable it means that he is capable of being good.

The man in black cracked his whip and the horses set off at a smart pace. Lapitch, Gita and the other boys and girls looked after them.

One of the herdboys said: 'They're going so fast you'd think their consciences were troubling them.'

'Let them go as fast as they like,' Lapitch said. 'I don't want to meet that man in the black coat again.'

'Well, if the world is as big as you say it is, I don't suppose you will,' observed Gita.

'When I began to look for my boots it seemed enormous. But now, when I'm afraid of meeting the man in black again, it seems quite a little place,' said Lapitch.

They all went and sat round the fire. Lapitch took out his meat and cake and as there were seven of them his bag was soon empty and no longer looked like a bumble-bee.

The night in the chimney corner

Lapitch and Gita and the herders talked for a long time about everything that had happened. Soon, night began to fall and it was time to take the cows home.

But the children had so much to talk about and were so comfortable round the fire that they never noticed what time it was.

The largest white cow then came up to little Mishko and licked his bare feet.

She wanted to say, 'Let's go home, Mishko.'

Mishko looked up and realized that the sun had set.

'Why, it's dark already!' he cried. All the others jumped up and began to herd the cows as quickly as they could.

'Where are we going?' Gita asked Lapitch.

Lapitch didn't know. It was too late to go on the road again but they had no shelter for the night. Lapitch was in trouble.

But Gita thought of something. Earlier in the day she had seen Lapitch with his awl and twine, and it had crossed her mind that they might be very useful.

'Offer to mend all their sandals at home,' she whispered, 'and perhaps they'll let us stay for the night.'

Lapitch did so, but he was a bit ashamed because he felt he should have thought of the idea himself.

However, the herders offered to put them up for the night, and so all of them went to the village which was not very far away.

The cows went first, their bells jingling. After them went Bundash, who kept them in order just as though he had been a real herd dog. After him walked the five herders and Lapitch and Gita.

Lapitch carried Gita's parrot on his shoulder because he had made great friends with it. The parrot had heard the name 'Gregory' so many times that day that the name had stuck to its tongue. So because parrots carry what they learn on their tongues rather than in their heads, the bird shouted 'Good evening, Gregory' to everyone they met when they came to the village. And of course everybody laughed, those who were called Gregory and those who were not. Because of this, Lapitch and Gita made an impression as soon as they arrived.

The little procession entered a courtyard. Lapitch promised Mishko's parents that he would mend all the sandals in the house the next day, and they said that he and Gita could stay the night. But they would have given them shelter in any case because farmers are usually kind to poor children.

After supper, everybody went to bed.

The children slept in the chimney corner, which was broad and roomy, warm in winter and cool in summer. Even though four of them had to cram into it, they slept soundly. Gita's parrot was put in a basket hanging from a rafter.

'It's a green owl,' said Mishko. 'Its beak is like a witch's nose. I'm sure it could peck our hearts out while we were asleep.'

And Mishko's grandma felt the same way, so that was why the parrot had to be shut in the basket.

Before Lapitch fell asleep he tried to reckon up how far he was from Master Scowler. It was no great distance. He could have gone all the way back in one day although it had taken him five to get where he was now. The reason was that he could not travel very quickly when he had Gita with him. But he wouldn't have dreamed of abandoning her and going on alone with Bundash. He was quite pleased that they had not yet caught up with her master and the circus. Sooner or later, though, they *would* catch them up.

For some time, Lapitch lay in the chimney corner worrying.

Then he thought, What's the use of fretting? Gregory fell into the ditch right under my nose. If I had worried for ten years about where to find him and give him the handkerchief I'd never have thought of that.

So he fell asleep.

Everybody in the house slept soundly and, although Mishko and Grandma had been quite sure there was a witch in the basket that hung from the rafter, they slept more deeply than anybody else.

The sixth day of the journey

The little shoemaker and Yana the beggar

Lapitch rose from the chimney corner at dawn because he had a lot of work to do. But Mishko's father and mother were already out working. Nobody gets up earlier than farming people.

As soon as he got up, Lapitch clapped his hands and called to the children, 'Wake up and give me your sandals. No more sleeping now!'

The children got down from the chimney corner, sleepy and warm and ruffled like young birds from a nest.

In no time at all a whole heap of sandals lay in front of Lapitch.

I'd better get down to it, he thought.

The sun came up and Lapitch found a shady place in front of the house to lay out his tools.

As soon as he began his work, he thought of nothing else but the job he was doing.

Gita disliked the very thought of hard work so she left him to it and went with the village girls to jump over the linen which the women spread on the grass to bleach. Of course she jumped better than any of them because she had done nothing else but jumping in the circus. She jumped over three rows of linen and then fell down in the middle of the fourth. Happily, its owner was not there to see her.

Lapitch worked and Gita played and presently Yana the beggar-woman came to the village.

When she saw Lapitch she was surprised to see that such a little shoemaker in such high boots had opened his workshop in the village. She said, 'Will you mend poor old Yana's sandals?'

'Of course I will! After all, the emperor has sent me on a journey through this country to give help where help is needed,' said Lapitch.

'If that's true it would be a good thing if he sent more such people,' said the old woman.

'They've been looking for more but nobody wanted to come except Lapitch the apprentice, and that's me.'

All this was nonsense of course but it made old Yana laugh and Lapitch started on her sandals right away.

And Yana sat down and talked as he did so, and told him everything that had happened in the last three villages she had walked through.

'Travel only during the day, my son. Last night something bad happened in the woods near here. Some people robbed a man who was taking his goods to a fair. Nobody knows whether he is alive or dead and the robbers went away in his cart.'

Lapitch didn't like that. When you travel you don't want to hear about horrible things that have happened to other travellers. But what old Yana told him was true. She went everywhere and knew everything.

At the fair

In the afternoon Lapitch said to Gita: 'It's high time we were off. We've got a long way to go and we must look for your master.'

'I've changed my mind, Lapitch,' said Gita. 'I don't want to go back to him.'

When Lapitch heard that he was delighted. He knew that it meant that he would have to look after her, but at least he would not be alone.

Lapitch and Gita said goodbye to Mishko and his brother, thanked their parents and went on their way.

They walked quickly and soon arrived in a large town.

It was so big that it had a church with two steeples and ten small ones with one steeple each. It had a hundred streets and people milling around in them like ants. Every street had four corners and at each one there stood two guards.

But Lapitch and Gita did not explore the hundred streets. They walked down one of them and found themselves in a big market-place, where a fair was in progress.

At the fair there were two hundred stalls, large and small. You could buy red handkerchiefs, black coats, blue pottery and yellow melons.

There was a great beating of drums and shrilling of whistles because many people were buying toys as well.

'Oh, isn't it fun here!' said Gita. 'Can't we stay for a while?'

There! I knew she would say that as soon as she laid eyes on the fair, thought Lapitch, but he said gently, not wishing to disappoint her: 'I don't think it would be a good thing to stay here long.'

'Why not?' demanded Gita.

'Because Master Scowler might be here. He doesn't usually go to fairs, but a few days before I left him I heard him say, "I'll go to the next fair. Surely fairs won't always mean misfortune for me."'

'Why should fairs mean misfortune for him?' asked Gita.

'I don't know, but he used to say that his misfortune came from a fair. It wouldn't be wise to stay here. We might meet him – we might even meet the man in black. And who knows, perhaps your master is here, with his circus.'

Gita tossed her head. 'Why should *all* of them be here?'

'Because there are crowds of people and, where there are crowds, there might be everybody.'

'Nonsense!' scoffed Gita. 'There are many more people in Vienna than there are here, but Master Scowler and the man in black are not in Vienna.'

Lapitch was not so good at words as Gita, so he preferred not to argue with her.

They stayed at the fair. Whether they had been wise to do so or not they were not to know until the evening. And until then there was so much noise that they couldn't possibly think of what might happen later.

The basket-makers

At first Gita and Lapitch certainly had a lovely and most interesting time at the fair. They arrived at a place where there was much more noise than anywhere else. Here, there were two basket-makers.

One of them had a big stall, striped blue and white. In it were rows of baskets, as yellow as gold. Above them hung more rows of baskets, red and blue, large and small, speckled and gilded. Right in the middle of them was a huge hamper large enough to hold a man.

'Come buy, come buy!' called the basket-maker, standing in front of the stall. 'Baskets, baskets! Made of gold and tied with silk!'

Of course, people came swarming around him like bees, attracted by the noise he was making and the sight of so much gold paint.

Not far away, the other basket-maker sat on the ground. Because he was poor he didn't have a stall so he sat on a sack. Round him stood about ten simple unpainted baskets. They were all he had. He did not say anything because he didn't know how to boast. But he was sad about having no customers because he had a lot of hungry children at home.

Whenever anyone went near him to look at his wares, the man in the other stall would call out: 'Don't stop there, come here! Don't buy those poor things. Your neighbours will say you found them on a dustheap! Come and look at *my* baskets, made of gold!'

And they all left the poor man and went to buy the other baskets.

Gita and Lapitch watched all this for some time. Gita, who had a good heart and could put things into words, said: 'I wish his stall could be struck by lightning and that big basket fall on top of him!'

They saw crowds of women flocking to the stall.

'Come buy, come buy!' shouted the man. 'My baskets are like golden apples!' And he whirled them about on their strings.

'Lapitch!' exclaimed Gita. 'I've got a wonderful idea! Quick, give me your knife. Oh, this is going to be fun!'

She thrust her hand into Lapitch's bag and took out the knife. Then she scuttled off like a squirrel and hid behind the stall.

What is she up to? wondered Lapitch.

Ah! You should have seen it! The women were crowding round the stall when suddenly the baskets hanging on the rope above the man's head started pelting down.

First one, then four, then ten! *Clitter-clatter* – golden and white, blue and speckled, down they came.

The rope on which they were hanging had broken.

'Ow! ow!' shouted the basket-maker and madly tried to ward off the baskets with his arms.

But then – *snap* – another rope went!

Another shower of baskets came down – *blip, clatter, crash* – onto

the man's head and shoulders. He was jumping around, waving his hands and yelling at the top of his voice, until he fell over.

There he was, rolling on the ground, struggling to get up again and shrieking, 'Ow! ouch!'

Then came a final crash. The huge hamper came down right on top of the man and covered him up. You couldn't see him at all. Only his hands and feet stuck out from under the hamper.

As the basket-maker scrambled about under the hamper, wildly waving his hands and feet, he sent the small baskets flying in all directions.

People were screaming with laughter, but nobody knew what had happened.

Gita crouched behind the stall, peering through a hole in the canvas. She was laughing more than anybody else because it was she who had cut the ends of both ropes with Lapitch's knife.

Lapitch knelt beside her and peeped through a hole too. As soon as the baskets had begun to fall he had guessed the reason and run to join her.

He would never have played a trick like that himself, but when he saw the basket-maker rolling among his yellow baskets like a big black beetle he laughed so much that his bag shook on his back. Gita had to put her hands over her mouth because she was shrieking with laughter.

'We'd better make ourselves scarce,' said Gita. 'While he is rolling about, we will sell the poor man's baskets.'

She ran over to the other basket-maker and said: 'If you'll let me try I'll sell everything you have.'

She took the tin plate which he had brought for the money – it was still empty – and beat it with a piece of wood, shouting: 'Baskets, baskets! Come buy!'

She put one of the baskets on her shoulder and her parrot perched on it. The bird also shrieked: 'Baskets, baskets!' and Gita beat the plate with all her might.

At once the customers gathered. As soon as there was a parrot screeching and a plate being beaten, people suddenly realized that the unpainted baskets were better and sturdier than the gold ones. This sort of thing happens at fairs and elsewhere. The women snapped them up one after the other. Gita and Lapitch sold all the baskets before the other man managed to scramble out from underneath the big hamper.

The poor man wondered, laughed and rejoiced. He stared at Gita, and seeing her beautiful long hair he thought she must be an angel sent from heaven to help him.

Gita poured all the money into the tin plate and gave it to the poor basket-maker. How he thanked them!

He invited both of them to pass the night at his poor home. But Lapitch and Gita wanted to spend more time at the fair so they thanked him but said no.

'We'd better go now and get away from the man in the other stall!' suggested Lapitch.

So Lapitch and Gita disappeared in the crowds.

The poor man counted the money in his tin plate; it came to exactly sixty crowns.

'I wish those children well!' he said to himself.

If he had known what was waiting for Lapitch and Gita he would certainly have insisted on taking them home with him!

On the merry-go-round

The voices of the traders were getting hoarse. At a fair this means that evening is approaching. Lapitch and Gita came to a place where there were merry-go-rounds and shooting galleries.

The gayest merry-go-round was made of silver and was covered with thousands of tiny bells. But it wasn't working, because the owner's two servants had left him. One of them had been supposed to sell tickets, the other to shout to people to come and ride on the wooden horses and swans: and both of them had to ride on the merry-go-round all the time.

Their master could not do all those things by himself, because he was very fat and it would have made him sick.

'Good,' said Gita. 'Let's offer to do the work for him, and then we'll get food and beds for the night.'

They did so and when the owner of the merry-go-round saw Lapitch in his green trousers and gay cap and Gita in her silver-ribboned dress, with her parrot on her shoulder, he was very pleased. He thought they looked exactly right for the work and immediately took them on. He went to start the engine while Lapitch and Gita each mounted a wooden horse. There was the sound of a trumpet: *tra! tra!* and the merry-go-round began to turn, with a great jingling of bells. It was most exciting! Gita stood up on her horse, waved her hand and bowed to right and left while Lapitch cried: 'Walk up, walk up! Only two cents a ride!' and they were going round merrily, as quick as lightning.

No other merry-go-round had a beautiful girl and a boy dressed in such gay clothes and shining boots, so the people all flocked to the silver one.

The merriment went on until late into the night. Everybody had fun, but the best time of all was had by the owner of the merry-go-round because he collected a bagful of money. Lapitch kept running to him with plates of coins. That evening Lapitch had so many goes on the merry-go-round that certainly no apprentice ever had so many. Even a journeyman couldn't afford to pay for all those turns. Bundash sat watching him, wondering why he kept going round and round and round.

It became very late but everybody loses all sense of time on a merry-go-round. Lapitch and Gita were quite startled when the engine suddenly stopped and the owner called out in a deep voice: 'Thank you, one and all. It's eleven o'clock and that's all for tonight. We'll be here tomorrow.'

The crowd melted away and the owner brought out a huge piece of canvas. He and Lapitch and Gita wrapped it round the merry-go-round, covering the thousand jingle bells and all the swans and horses.

When they had finished it looked like a big, grey mushroom.

Then the owner took the children to a tent where they sold food.

By now, the people at the fair were thinning out. Only a few men with long moustaches were sitting in the tent.

Gita and Lapitch didn't like the fair very much at night.

The owner ordered supper and the three of them, Gita, Lapitch and Bundash, ate in silence because they felt rather tired and sad.

When they had finished, the master paid the bill and they all went back to the merry-go-round. Then he said: 'Goodbye children, be off with you and thank you very much.'

Lapitch and Gita were taken aback and felt rather helpless. They had supposed the owner would find somewhere for them to sleep.

Lapitch mentioned this, but the owner said that inside the merry-go-round there was only one bed for himself and no room for them.

This was indeed true, because he was so fat he could barely stretch out near the engine.

'And I don't let anyone sleep near the wooden animals,' he said severely, adding: 'It's not cold outside and the fairground is very large. You can go wherever you like. Goodbye and good night.'

Then he disappeared under the canvas.

So Gita, Lapitch, Bundash and the parrot were all alone in the dark, in the midst of the great fairground.

Nobody was about and the only sound that broke the stillness was snoring from the travelling folk, who lay sleeping by their wares.

It was really sad and horrid. Such a big town, a hundred streets and a hundred houses to each of them, and yet Lapitch and Gita stood outside without a roof to their heads and there was nowhere they could ask for shelter.

Homeless

Lapitch looked at Gita. It was dark but he could just see that her head drooped and she was stroking her dress.

He knew very well that this was a sign that she was going to cry and if she did he would hardly be able to bear it. So he said cheerfully: 'Don't be frightened, it's a lovely warm night. We'll sleep out and we'll have so much air we shan't need to open the windows! Come on, let's find somewhere.'

He remembered that not very far away there was a pile of empty sacks and rags. He led Gita towards the place where he thought it was. They couldn't see a thing and as they groped around, Gita sighed: 'Oh, if only we had gone with the basket-maker!'

'Well, if we had we wouldn't have had so many rides on the merry-go-round,' Lapitch pointed out. They both cheered up remembering what fun it had been when they had whirled round and round to the sound of all the little bells.

Lapitch found the heap of sacks and rags and arranged them as best he could.

'Lie down,' he said to Gita, 'and you'll sleep like the princess on the pea, see if you don't!'

Gita put the parrot beside her and lay down on the sacks.

Lapitch and Bundash lay side by side on the ground.

Bundash whined sadly, not because of himself – he was used to sleeping on the ground – but because of Lapitch.

They all felt so downhearted that Gita and Lapitch decided to talk.

'What did you mean about the princess on the pea?' asked Gita.

She loved to hear stories about princesses, even in the daytime, and she particularly wanted to hear one now, when everything was so dark and horrid. So Lapitch told the story.

'Once upon a time there was a princess who lost her way and came to a golden castle. It really was pure gold, the steps and the threshold and everything. An old queen lived there but she didn't believe that her visitor was a real princess. So she put a dried pea in the princess's bed and three straw mattresses and nine eiderdowns on top of it. She thought that if the girl felt the pea through all that she must surely be a real princess. The next day, the old queen asked the princess how she had slept. The princess burst into tears. "Alas", she said, "I tossed and turned all night and I am bruised all over! There was a hard hillock in my bed." So then the old queen knew she was a princess, because only a real princess could feel a pea under three straw mattresses and nine eiderdowns. And she gave her her throne and robe and her golden crown because she was old and ruling had given her a headache.'

After this lovely story with so many eiderdowns and a golden castle Gita and Lapitch felt better and didn't mind sleeping on the ground in the open air.

They fell asleep at exactly midnight, and so the sixth day of Lapitch's journey ended.

The seventh night was beginning – a night when extraordinary things happened. (But everywhere, every day, extraordinary things happen – more, in fact, than all the people in all the world ever invent.) For Lapitch this seventh night brought dangerous and amazing adventures.

But Lapitch, so small and so brave, is probably going to cope with any danger that comes.

The seventh night

A familiar voice

Hardly had Gita and Lapitch fallen asleep when Gita wakened up. In her sleep she had heard something which made her heart beat faster.

She sat up on her sacks and listened. Somewhere, a horse was neighing.

It neighed once. Gita thought she knew the sound.

It neighed a second time. Gita thought even more that she knew the sound. When it neighed a third time she jumped up and cried: 'Lapitch, oh Lapitch! Can you guess whose horse is neighing? Do let's go!'

By this time the moon had risen and they could see where they were.

Lapitch got up and he and Bundash and Gita went towards the place the sound was coming from.

Soon they arrived at a large piece of ground, bare except for a huge tent pitched in the middle of it. The tent was closed up and silent as if it were asleep, but on the doorflap there was a long red notice. It was Gita's circus!

'Oh, Lapitch, listen!' exclaimed Gita. 'I can hear Soko, my own dear, darling Soko!"

She had quite forgotten how frightened she was of the circus-master and that she did not want to go back to him. She only remembered the pony with which she had shared good and bad times, and which she loved better than anything else in the world. She simply couldn't resist trying to see him.

'Lapitch, I'm going in to see him,' she said.

'Then your boss will see you and we will have to part,' Lapitch pointed out sadly.

'Oh, no, we won't! I'm not going to stay there. They're all sleeping like logs because they're tired after the performance. They'll never hear us. Oh, please, please let's go in!'

They were standing right next to the stable which was made out of canvas and adjoined the tent.

Gita had plenty of experience, of course, in finding ways of getting into tents. She lifted up the canvas and whispered: 'Come on, under here!'

So she crawled into the stables, and Lapitch and Bundash followed.

This alone was foolhardy enough.

The circus at night

Near by, a man lay asleep on some straw.

'Don't worry,' Gita whispered, '*he* wouldn't wake up if you blew a trumpet in his ear! You can't think how deeply one sleeps after the show.'

A ring dangled from a pole: this was where Gita's parrot had always perched.

Gita put the parrot back there and when the bird realized that it was in its old place it thought: Everything is as it should be, and, quite content, it tucked its head under its wing and went to sleep.

But it was the only one that was happy.

Gita and Lapitch were taking a great risk! They edged past the sleeping man. A light was on in the stable and Lapitch saw four horses on each side: not a lot for a circus, perhaps, but he was most impressed.

'What a lot of horses and how beautiful they are!' he breathed.

But Gita was not listening. She had already found her pony.

'Soko, darling Soko!' she crooned to him, stroking his white back and putting her arms round his neck.

And Soko turned his beautiful little head and rested it on Gita's shoulder, neighing softly with joy.

'Darling, Soko, however can I leave you again?' whispered Gita.

Meanwhile, Lapitch went a little farther into the stable.

'That black horse is the loveliest one,' he murmured.

'But we haven't got any black horses,' protested Gita.

'But there *is* one, just come and look!'

Gita went to see and it was quite true! A lovely little horse was standing there, glossy and black as coal. His mane and tail were cut short and he wore beautiful yellow leg bandages.

Gita stared at him in amazement and at last she said: 'I'd never have believed it! This is the little black horse that pulled Gregory and the man in black, in their cart yesterday. He looks different because of his mane and tail having been clipped, and because of the leg bandages, but he's the same one!'

Lapitch couldn't believe it either, and they went up to the manger to look at him more closely.

And then their hearts missed a beat!

They heard somebody coming into the stable: they could hear men's deep voices and heavy boots crunching the sand on the floor.

'Oh, whatever shall we do?' wailed Gita softly. 'It's my boss and, oh Lapitch, I don't want to stay with him. I'm frightened!'

There was nothing else for them to do but hide under the black horse's manger.

Lapitch, Gita and Bundash crawled underneath. Lapitch pulled up some straw from under the black horse's hooves so that they were hidden.

Two men entered the stable.

More danger!

'Oh dear, oh dear! who can it be?' wondered Lapitch and Gita. They cowered under the manger, peeping through the straw. They were as quiet as mice but their hearts were thumping against their breasts.

When the men stood under the light and the children could see them, they were much more frightened. For the men were – the owner of the circus and the man in black!

How come they know each other and what are they doing here so late? thought Lapitch and Gita, more and more dismayed. They were in terrible danger, for the two men walked right up to the black horse. They came so close to Lapitch and Gita that there were only a few wisps of straw between them and the children. Oh, didn't they keep quiet! They breathed so softly that there was not the slightest rustle in the straw.

'Bundash, dear Bundash, don't bark!' breathed Lapitch into the dog's ear. He held Bundash tightly, for he felt him start when he saw the man in black. But Bundash was as good as gold and, because he could feel how Lapitch's hands were trembling, he didn't move a muscle.

Then the circus-master and the man in black started talking.

Two bad men

If Lapitch had not been so poor he would probably never have seen such a couple of villains at close quarters. It is a good thing that really wicked men are so few and far between: indeed, these two were the only ones in that particular district. But Lapitch was a poor child and poor children get to know the whole world.

'Tomorrow I shall travel through seven towns and pitch my tents in the eighth,' said the circus-owner. 'Look at the horse, haven't I done him up well? When he's properly saddled and harnessed nobody will recognize him.'

'I haven't the slightest fear they will – you're a cunning old fox!' said the man in black. 'But now you'd better give me the money. It wasn't easy to get hold of him, remember!'

'I'll pay you,' said the circus-master. 'But first, tell me, where is the horse's owner?'

'You needn't worry about *him.* He's in the depths of the forest, tied to the strongest oak tree I could find with three stout ropes. I tied him up myself so you may be sure he'll never get free. It'll be a long time before *he* visits a fair again.'

And the man in black laughed as evilly as only bad men can laugh when they talk about their wicked deeds.

Reassured, the circus-owner took out his heavy purse and counted out some gold coins into the robber's hands.

'I'll say goodbye now,' said the man in black. 'My cart is waiting for me and I must press on while it's dark.'

'Why are you in such a hurry?'

'Because we're going to steal a cow before dawn. I sent Gregory there last night, to wait for me. But I don't really trust him.'

'Whereabouts is the cow?'

'I haven't been there yet, but I believe it's at a house that stands by itself at the side of the road and only a woman and a child live there. So it will be very easy. But it will take three hours to drive there because I'm going by a roundabout way.'

'How will you find the house if you've never been there before?'

'Oh, quite easily. It's small, old and patched up and it has a big blue star painted on it.'

Then the two men left the stable. The children heard them say goodbye to each other outside, then all was quiet.

Lapitch makes a decision

Lapitch and Gita and Bundash crawled out from under the manger. Lapitch's head was buzzing! The man in black and Gregory had robbed that man who was going to the fair, taken his horses and tied him up in the woods! But Lapitch worried most of all because that night the men would go and take the cow belonging to Marko and his mother who were so poor! There could be no mistake: their cottage was certainly small and old, and surely no other place had a blue star painted on it?

So Lapitch said to Gita: 'Goodbye, Gita, I have to hurry. Stay with your boss and don't cry.'

But Gita burst into tears before he had finished.

'Lapitch, where are you going?'

'I've got to get to Marko's house before the man in black, to warn his mother to guard her cow.'

How kind and good Lapitch was – and what a long way he had to tramp on his little feet!

'Lapitch, it's an awfully long way and the man in black has a cart,' wailed Gita.

'I know, that's why I must hurry. Goodbye, Gita, it's better if you stay here.'

'I'm going with you,' said Gita firmly, drying her tears.

Lapitch had no time to talk any more. He just crawled with Bundash under the canvas and out into the moonlight. Gita went after him.

Lapitch didn't say anything. His boots went marching down the long town street at a good pace. Gita's little shoes came tapping behind him just as fast. But Bundash's four paws pattered fastest of all.

So they left the town, feeling that they were being watched from every window.

Before them was a long road which seemed endless.

The moon shone down on them and also on the little house with the blue star. Would they get there in time?

Walking at night

Some people say that the grass and flowers talk at night time. If it is true, then certainly all the meadows whispered that night, 'Oh, little children, why are you going in the middle of the night?'

But Lapitch never thought about how far he had to go, nor that the man in the cart would get there first. He only thought of reaching Marko's house before dawn. And that's the best way, for if you think like that your feet will surely get you there. So he walked on quickly and Gita soon got tired. After all, she did not know Marko, so she was not so anxious to help him as Lapitch was.

After a short while, she said: 'Lapitch, can't we rest a bit?'

She spoke softly because voices carry far in the stillness of the night.

'*I*'m not tired,' said Lapitch, 'and we've no time to stop. We must go on.' He had known it would be difficult if Gita came with him.

Gita sighed a little and they went on.

All the time she was thinking about the black horse, Gregory and the man in black, and she wondered how they had been able to bring the horse into the circus when there were so many guards in the town. She asked Lapitch how he thought they had managed it.

'Oh, well, guards seem to stand at the corners and criminals drive in the middle of the road,' said Lapitch.

This seemed a funny idea to Gita, but she thought that since Lapitch was an apprentice, he probably knew best. So she was silent.

In any case, it was not the time to talk. Walking through meadows in the middle of the night is like walking in a dream. Big night-moths flew past their heads beating their wings like birds. Gita saw an old hedgehog trotting beside them on the grass, and now and again in the meadows they caught a glimpse of hares' ears sticking out of the grass. They heard birds rustling in the bushes.

At night, animals are not so frightened of people because they know human beings are afraid of the dark and they are not.

Perhaps Lapitch and Gita would have been afraid of being all alone on the road. But they had Bundash, who ran in front of them waving his tail cheerfully and looking at Lapitch, as if to say: 'Don't worry, I know the way quite well.'

When they had gone quite a long way, Gita said: 'Lapitch, please do let us rest a little. I just can't go on.'

Indeed, her feet were smaller than Lapitch's and she was wearing silk shoes, whereas Lapitch wore his boots.

'Gita, we have a long way to go, we have to go through several villages and the crossroads.'

When Lapitch mentioned the crossroads, Gita remembered how at that spot yesterday, the horses had reared, overturning the cart and left the man in black lying in the ditch.

'Oh, Lapitch, what shall we do if the cart catches up with us?' she said and started sobbing.

Since Gita was in tears, of course it was impossible to go on. She sank down on the road and hid her face in her hands.

Lapitch stood by her and wondered what he should do. He could not leave Gita alone, but if she went with him he could not possibly reach Marko's house before dawn. Lapitch was sad, imagining the man in black stealing Marko's beautiful spotted cow. What shall I do? Whatever shall I do? he thought.

Dear heaven! Can't somebody come and help this little apprentice standing so sadly on the road in the middle of the night!

Out of the mist

Lapitch stood looking up and down the road. Towards the town he thought he saw something moving. But he could not see what it was because of the mist. He could only hear a soft, slow rumble.

At night time one is more inclined to expect enemies than friends.

That was exactly how Lapitch felt when he saw that a cart was approaching. He was uneasy. Gita cried: 'Oh, Lapitch, why did we ever start this journey in the dark?'

Only Bundash sniffed the air and seemed quite happy.

The cart came nearer and nearer and at last it seemed like a mountain coming down the road. In the mist everything seems three times bigger than it really is.

Now it was very near and they could see that the horse drawing it was very thin.

Suddenly, the mist cleared and the moon shone brighter and Lapitch and Gita shouted with joy.

The man driving the cart was the poor basket-maker from the fair!

Lapitch gets some help

In fact, this was no miracle. The basket-maker did not drive that way because Lapitch and Gita were standing there on the road in the middle of the night and needed help. He used to drive that way very often when they weren't there at all.

He usually went far out of the town to get really good willow twigs. That was why his baskets were stronger and better than any others.

Lapitch, Gita and Bundash ran up to him. When the basket-maker saw them on the road in the moonlight he decided that they really had come down from heaven and that they probably travelled by night so that they could help poor people in the day time.

But Lapitch himself needed help now and he asked the basket-maker to give them a lift.

The poor man was delighted to help the children who had been so kind to him at the fair. So Lapitch and Gita climbed up behind him and the basket-maker touched his scrawny horse with his whip.

Lapitch told his story.

'So you see I must be at the house with the blue star before dawn.'

'Oh, I know where that is,' said the basket-maker. 'It's quite near my willow grove. I'll show you the way and you'll be there long before the dawn.'

Lapitch was delighted, and suddenly the way seemed quite short.

The scrawny horse went quickly and well, just as though he knew something important was at stake.

The cart jolted along. Lapitch and the basket-maker talked, Gita

dozed and Bundash ran cheerfully along the road, sometimes by the right wheel, sometimes by the left one, as it has always been since dogs and wheels began.

At last they came to the crossroads.

'We will go this way, uphill and through the woods. It's a short cut,' the basket-maker told Lapitch.

'Oh, not that way,' cried Gita, waking up. 'Those are the woods where a man was robbed.'

But the basket-maker knew the countryside quite well and didn't take any notice of her. He said: 'This is a much shorter way to my willow grove. You needn't be frightened. I've never met a robber there yet.' The basket-maker was very poor, and poor people aren't afraid of robbers.

So they drove towards the woods.

Lapitch was pleased because it meant that he would get to Marko's house sooner. And anyone who is going to someone's help isn't afraid of anything except being late.

Lapitch and Gita alone again

The beginning of the road was uphill and then they entered the wood. The sky was cloudless just then and the moonlight so bright that it lit up the forest as though it were a castle with candles in all the windows.

When they came out of the trees Lapitch noticed that they were on the top of a little hill.

Here the basket-maker stopped the cart and said: 'Children, you must go to the left to get to the cottage with the blue star. You will pass through a thicket and when you have left that behind you will see the house.'

Looking up, he saw a big cloud coming up and added: 'You will be clear of the trees before that cloud hides the moon.'

Gita wanted to cry out that she would be frightened if he left them all alone again.

But Lapitch jumped down from the cart and thanked the basket-maker for his help.

The basket-maker lifted Gita down and saying 'God speed you, dear children' took the road to the right downhill, and Lapitch said, 'Come on, we go downhill to the left.'

There was no time for Gita to protest.

So she and Lapitch and Bundash were alone again and went down the road which lay between the wood and the thicket. As they started out, they heard the basket-maker's voice.

'Children,' he called, 'look out for the quarry!'

And sure enough, right beside them, there was a sheer drop where stone had been quarried. It was a dangerous place because your foot could easily slip in the dark and you would fall down the cliff. However, the moonlight was so bright that they got round it safely. Lapitch was pleased and excited because he knew that soon they would reach Marko's house.

'All will be right if the moon stays bright,' the basket-maker had said.

Darkness in the thicket

You never know what to expect from clouds, they behave as they please.

Until they reached the thicket, Lapitch and Gita could see their way as in daylight.

But as soon as they were in the midst of it, the light became weaker and weaker. Clouds were sailing over the moon.

The path was narrow and the children could hardly see it.

We must go on, Lapitch told himself – it's quite easy to see, really.

As soon as he reassured himself in this way it did seem as though he saw better.

Gita followed him, because she couldn't make out a thing in the dark. And Bundash went in front of both of them.

But then a cloud completely covered the moon and it was really impossible to see anything at all.

Lapitch groped to find the path. Thorns and twigs caught at Gita's dress.

'We'd better stop,' said Lapitch at last. 'We might get lost and that wouldn't do at all.'

This was very sad because he knew he had to hurry to Marko.

But Lapitch didn't like being miserable. He looked up at the sky and hoped that the cloud would soon go, and thought that, in any case, they couldn't be very far from the house with the blue star.

'We'll sit down and wait a little,' he told Gita.

So they sat down on a tree-stump and waited in the darkness and silence. All round them in the thicket there were birds: blackbirds, titmice and wild pigeons. But they too kept quiet like Lapitch and Gita because they were afraid of foxes.

At last Lapitch burst out: 'Oh, if I can only get to Marko's house in time!'

'And if only the man in black weren't going too!' sighed Gita.

'He said he would go a roundabout way and this is a short cut,' Lapitch pointed out.

Just then, it seemed to Lapitch and Gita that the silence was not as complete as before. Behind them, at the other end of the thicket, something rustled.

'Oh, Lapitch, whatever is that?' whispered Gita.

'A rabbit, perhaps,' said Lapitch.

He got up from the tree-stump and kept Bundash close by him.

Then they could hear dry sticks cracking.

'Oh, Lapitch, Lapitch, what *is* it?' whispered Gita even lower in the darkness.

'May be a fox,' said Lapitch.

'That's no fox,' breathed Gita, as softly as a ghost.

'Then it is . . .' Lapitch began to say.

But suddenly Gita screamed at the top of her voice: 'Lapitch, Lapitch!'

Quite close to her, a man coughed.

Terror

As soon as Gita screamed, the rustling and cracking stopped at once.

That was even more terrifying. The silence, the darkness and knowing that somewhere near them was a man whom they did not know –

it was all horrible! Only Bundash tugged at Lapitch and quivered with excitement.

Then, suddenly, there were more sounds of branches breaking and in the darkness the children could just see a very tall man come out onto the path. Their hearts stood still – then they heard the man strike a match.

The match flared up——

Well, if you've read this book so far and if you're fond of Lapitch perhaps you'd better close this book now and wait until tomorrow!

A surprise

As the match flared up, Lapitch was able to see the man's face.

It was Master Scowler! He was deathly pale and his clothes were torn. He stood there and exclaimed in his deep voice: 'Lapitch! Is it really you?'

'Yes, sir,' said Lapitch, and held out both his hands. He did not know whether he was glad or afraid.

And what do you think Master Scowler did?

What *do* you think?

He came right up to Lapitch, lifted him up and said: 'Lapitch, my dear little boy!'

And for the first time in his life, he stroked Lapitch's hair and face!

Lapitch was more astonished at this than at anything that had happened to him that night or in his life. Probably nothing that ever happens to him will surprise him more!

It was no wonder that both he and Master Scowler cried a little with joy, although, as they were both men, they did not usually give way to tears.

Explanations

They sat down on the tree-stump, all three of them, Lapitch, Master Scowler and Gita.

They were all so stunned with amazement that at first they did not know what to do or say. It seemed that the very moon, just coming out of the clouds, must be surprised to see who was sitting on that tree-stump.

Only Bundash didn't think that anything was extraordinary. He put his front paws on Lapitch's knees and looked first at him and then at Master Scowler. He thought they must both be here to make shoes, and he waited for Master Scowler to produce his leather and scissors. Dogs seldom understand anything new, only things that have happened often.

Master Scowler then began to explain how he had come to be in the woods, and what a story it was! Lapitch sat there, his little apprentice's head in a whirl. To save the reader from feeling the way Lapitch did, we will cut the story short.

Two days ago, Master Scowler had been robbed when he was driving through the woods to the fair. He was the man that Yana had mentioned to Lapitch. This was how it had happened.

Master Scowler had set off at daybreak alone in the cart because the man from whom he had hired the horses had gone ahead of him with another cart.

When he reached the thickest part of the woods, two men had ambushed him. They sprang out of the trees, pulled him from the cart, bound his wrists and led him deep into the forest. There they tied him to a tree and then drove off, leaving him to starve.

For two whole days Master Scowler remained tied to the tree, and as he was quite sure that there was no help for him, he commended his soul to God. He remembered everything he had done in his life, good and evil, and he also remembered Lapitch and longed to see him once more. When a man is tied to a tree for two days without food or drink, he has plenty of time to ponder, and the way he thinks about his apprentice then is quite different from when he is shouting at him in the workshop.

Anyway, as he told the children, he had given up hope and decided that he would never get away from the tree alive.

'Then last night,' he continued, 'one of the two men who had tied me up came to me. I thought he had come to kill me, but instead he untied my ropes and said: "Go now, with the help of God, and get out of these woods quickly."

'And he took a handkerchief out of his pocket and there was a silver coin wrapped up in it. He gave it to me and said: "Take this. Since I got it, my heart has turned from evil to good. Perhaps it will bring happiness to you too. I am going away to lead a better life."'

When Master Scowler had finished, Lapitch exclaimed: 'Oh, that was Gregory! I took him the silver coin from his mother! She didn't weep for him in vain.'

'She certainly didn't,' said Master Scowler. 'It must be a coin that works miracles.'

It occurred to Lapitch that perhaps it was the coin that was making Master Scowler kind to him. He rather hoped so, because he had already wondered whether the change was only due to his master having been tied to a tree without anything to eat or drink.

When Master Scowler ended his story, he added: 'You see, because of the fair, misfortune almost came to me for the second time.'

'What happened the first time?'

'I'll tell you all about it when we get home. Because now, my dear little Lapitch, you must come back with me and you will be happy, so don't worry. I can't talk any more now. I'm very hungry, because all I've had to eat was a little piece of dry bread I had in my pocket – I managed to quench my thirst at the stream.'

By this time, the clouds had gone and it was clear moonlight again. Master Scowler looked at Gita who sat there quietly, and he thought she was like a small, beautiful, frightened bird.

'And who is this?' he asked.

'She's an orphan, like me. She hasn't any father or mother so we travel together,' said Lapitch.

'We'll take her home with us,' said Master Scowler, and it seemed to his apprentice that he suddenly looked very sad.

Then Lapitch jumped up and cried: 'Oh, dear, how much time I've lost! The moon is bright now so let's hurry to Marko's house.'

'We'll go together,' said Master Scowler. 'I don't like this forest. On the way you can tell me where you are going and why you have to hurry.'

At Marko's house

Soon they reached the end of the thicket. Master Scowler gave one hand to Lapitch and the other to Gita and of course it was quite lovely to walk like that through meadows in the moonlight. As they walked, Lapitch told him about the man in black and Marko's cow.

Then they came onto the road and saw Marko's house. All was quiet as they approached it and nothing dreadful seemed to have happened. They could hear the sound of a bell from the cowshed. Inside it the beautiful spotted cow was nibbling hay.

So the man in black had not yet taken her away! Lapitch was delighted because he had arrived in time!

It was not yet dawn. Inside the house everything was silent. Marko and his mother were still asleep.

Then Lapitch knocked at the door, and Marko's mother got up and came to see who was there.

Lapitch told her why he had come and warned her to guard her cow.

When she heard what he had to say, she raised her hands to heaven three times and thanked God for sending Lapitch to her.

For if the man in black had taken her cow, all she would have had left would have been ten geese. And a mother with a child cannot make a living with only ten geese.

'A thousand thanks, dear child,' she said, and hugged Lapitch, who said goodbye to her and went back to where Master Scowler and Gita were waiting for him.

Marko's mother put on her best dress and went to the district office to get a guard to come at night.

Two guards came to keep watch on her little house every night. Guards are very brave and when they are there no harm will come to anybody.

But the man in black did not come that night, nor the night after, nor even the night after that. In fact he never came at all. Every night, the guards smoked three pipes of tobacco and when they had smoked thirty they decided it was safe enough for them not to come again.

After a few days, a body was found. A man had fallen, probably in the dark, into the deep quarry about which the basket-maker had warned Lapitch and Gita.

The dead man was dressed in a black coat. It was the man in black whose evil life had finished thus.

He had fallen down the cliff when the cloud covered the moon.

So that same cloud which had dismayed Lapitch and Gita so much was lucky for them and Marko's mother and Master Scowler. If it had not come when it did, perhaps the man in black would have killed all of them. It shows that one should always wait a little before one starts sighing.

Now, for Lapitch all danger was past. What comes next is nothing but joy and happiness – such great joy as he never would have thought of eight days ago when he had run away in the night, so lonely and so sad.

Home again

Happy return

There is not much point in telling how Master Scowler, Lapitch, Gita and Bundash got back to Master Scowler's house. Happy people do not notice how far they have to go.

But on the way, Lapitch gathered a bunch of wild flowers – red poppies and white daisies – and that was all that happened.

So they came to the town, then to the master's house, then into the courtyard. Then they went into the house.

How Master Scowler's wife cried out with joy when she saw her husband and Lapitch and Bundash. She had thought she would never see any of them again. She had heard that her husband had been robbed and taken into the forest and she had supposed that he must be dead.

So she was wearing a black kerchief on her head, and her eyes were red with crying.

But now they had all come back and brought a beautiful little girl with them! She greeted Gita so kindly and looked at her so tenderly that the child's heart felt as though there was some wonderful happiness in store for her.

Then they all went into the workshop. We shall leave them there for a time so that they can hug and kiss one another, have something to eat and recover from the hardships of the journey.

Maritsa

A little later, Master Scowler, his wife, Lapitch and Gita were sitting at the table. They were rested and refreshed now, so their faces were happy and quiet.

Only the master's wife still looked at Gita tenderly and her expression was a little sad. At last she said to her husband: 'Our Maritsa would be about Gita's age now.'

Both of them sighed and then Master Scowler said to Lapitch: 'I promised to tell you of the misfortune that befell us at the fair, so now you shall hear about it. Eight years ago, we lived in another town and we had a beautiful little daughter called Maritsa. She was three years old and the joy of our lives. One day there was a fair in that town and I went there and took her with me. While I was selling my shoes she got lost in the crowd. We searched and searched for her the whole day but the child had vanished. We searched the whole day, and the week through, and the month that followed and the whole year round. But we never found our little Maritsa again. There were all kinds of people there. God knows what evil person took her away and how much she had to suffer – and we too! We suffered because whatever a child feels, its parents feel also. In the end we moved from that town because we didn't want to be reminded of the place where such a terrible thing happened to us. And from that time, my dear Lapitch, I hardened my heart and you had to suffer very much because of this. But now things will be different. For if you had not been kind, Gregory would never have repented and helped me to escape.'

Lapitch did not know where to look when Master Scowler praised him. He fidgeted, first scratching his ear and then wiping his boots with the sleeve of his red shirt. Then he said: 'I suppose you couldn't find Maritsa – and if you did you probably wouldn't know her now?'

'We shall never find her,' said the master's wife, sorrowfully, wiping away a tear. 'But we should still know her.'

'How would you know her now, since she was so little when you last saw her?' asked Gita. She was nearly crying herself because this kind and gentle lady was so sad.

'We would know her,' said Master Scowler's wife, 'because when she was very small she grabbed at a knife and cut her thumb. It made a scar shaped like a cross.'

My, my! Have you ever seen a mother and child hug when they are reunited after many years!

For Gita had that scar on her thumb – she, of course, was Maritsa!

'Mother, darling mother! I am your Maritsa!' she cried, and flung herself into Mrs Scowler's arms.

'Oh, my dearest Maritsa! My own darling!' The master's wife wept from sheer happiness and hugged her daughter.

They hugged twice and three times and ten times. All you could hear in the room was Mrs Scowler sobbing with joy.

Master Scowler went up to Gita and laid his hand on her head, and was so happy that he could not say a single word. Their joy seemed to flood the room with golden light.

Our good little Lapitch felt as though he were in church. He stood quite still, his eyes cast down and his hands joined.

They sat and talked for a long time afterwards and Gita went from her mother to her father, and the more they looked at her the more beautiful she seemed to them. And to her, her parents seemed to grow more wonderful every minute.

Of course, she was really Maritsa, and that is what her parents called her. But we shall call her Gita until the end of the story, because it is difficult to get used to a new name.

And Lapitch said: 'I shall go on calling you Gita, because when I say it I think of all the adventures we had together. When I say Maritsa it seems as though I'm talking to a stranger.'

'You certainly had enough adventures, dear Lapitch,' said Gita's father. 'I suppose we shall never know who took away our Maritsa at the fair and gave her to the circus. Who knows – perhaps it was the man in black, the thief who took the black horse, as you have been telling me. Ah, Lapitch – without you Maritsa would never have seen us again!'

'I don't deserve to be praised,' said Lapitch. 'If you had not been so strict with me I should never have run away and found your daughter. So perhaps it's all through you, really.'

Lapitch was right. You cannot always tell who really deserves praise. So when two people praise one another, they had better give thanks to God.

And this is what they did.

The next day, Master Scowler and his wife bought new clothes for both the children and then they all went to church, dressed in their best. Joyful sunshine fell on them through the church windows. It made them feel they had done the right thing in coming there to give thanks.

Lapitch's legacy

When they came back from church, Lapitch said: 'There is still something I must do. Please may I go out for half an hour?'

Of course Master Scowler let him go, because now everything was very different from the time when poor Lapitch had had to make a joke of the green trousers he disliked so much.

So Lapitch took the bunch of poppies and daisies he had gathered on the way, and explained that he had promised it to somebody.

Now you see how kind Lapitch was. In spite of all his adventures, he had not forgotten that he had promised some flowers to the maid if she helped the old milkman by carrying the heavy milk-can upstairs for him.

So now he set out with the bouquet for her. He soon found the house. Climbing up to the third floor he rang the bell.

The maid opened the door and was very surprised to see the funny Lapitch dressed in such lovely clothes. Still, she knew at once, for you don't know a person by his dress, but by his eyes.

'I promised you these, miss,' said Lapitch, giving her the daisies and poppies.

'I must say you're a man of your word,' said the maid, 'and you're lucky too. I've got a letter for you, and if you hadn't brought the flowers you'd never have got it.'

Lapitch had had many adventures on his journey, but he never had a letter in his life.

He was quite dumbfounded when the maid went into her room and came out again with a large envelope.

'A boy brought this,' she said. 'He told me the milkman had died from old age. Before his death he had written this. And the boy said that if Lapitch the apprentice brought me my flowers I should give it to him.'

Lapitch took the letter and turned it over and over in his hands. He really didn't know what to do with it and he wondered whether he should give it to the maid as a present along with the flowers. But then he thought that this would be silly, because on the letter it said 'To Lapitch the apprentice' and I am the only person in the world called that.

So he opened the letter right away.

It was the right thing to do. If you are worrying about the contents of a letter, do as Lapitch did, for a closed letter is always much more worrying than an open one.

However, this letter was a wonderful one. It was printed in large letters and it said:

'The old milkman had no children or relatives or godparents. When he died, he remembered Lapitch the apprentice and left his donkey and cart to him. This is to tell Lapitch the apprentice to come to the old man's house by the town toll-bar to collect his inheritance.'

At the top and bottom there were things written and numbers and probably the signature of the person who had written this and his address, but Lapitch didn't read that either at that moment or ever. He was too full of gratitude.

'Oh, how I wish I could thank the old man!' he exclaimed. 'How I wish he could know how well Gita and I will look after his donkey! Goodbye, miss,' he said to the maid. 'I must run back and tell Gita the good news!'

He was just about to run downstairs when the old lady of the house came out of her room, an old and very distinguished-looking person, wearing a black silk dress and a small white cap on her head.

She was the maid's employer and she had heard from her what a good and unusual boy Lapitch was.

She offered to adopt him and send him to a good school.

Lapitch took off his cap, kissed her hand and said: 'Dear madam, you are very kind. But if you don't mind, I would rather be a shoe-

maker because I like the trade.' And he added, 'As it is, many more people wear out shoes than mend them.'

The old lady laughed and agreed that it would be a great pity if Lapitch did not become a shoemaker. So he kissed her hand again and ran downstairs with his letter.

Lapitch certainly did like making shoes, but at the moment all he could think about was his donkey. And if he had accepted the old lady's offer he would have had nowhere to put it.

He ran through the streets and was at home in next to no time.

'We'll be able to take the shoes round with our donkey and cart,' he shouted to Master Scowler, waving his letter. And he told him what had happened.

So that afternoon, he and Gita went to collect the old milkman's legacy. They might have had difficulty finding his house but the directions in the letter said it was near the town toll-bar. The toll-bar sticks up high in the air and can easily be seen.

When Lapitch showed them the letter, the people who had shared the milkman's house handed over the donkey and cart.

So he and Gita had a wonderful ride through the town, and Gita only regretted that she hadn't her golden trumpet to blow! After all, she had grown up in a circus!

But Lapitch pointed out that it would not be suitable for Master Scowler's daughter to blow a trumpet, riding on a donkey through the town. So they just sang cheerfully and now and again cracked the whip, while the donkey pricked up his long ears.

As soon as they got home, though, Lapitch couldn't help showing how happy he was. He jumped down from the cart, throwing his cap in the air, and ran to the house.

He put his head round the door and shouted at the top of his voice, 'Here's the donkey!'

Gita burst out laughing.

'Do you mean yourself?' she asked.

So to avoid any more mix-ups of this kind, they gave the donkey a name: Kokodan.

A woman stood nearby, and when she saw Lapitch and Gita so happy she sighed and said: 'Wouldn't it be lovely if children stayed that age for ever!'

'If we did,' said Lapitch, 'we should be in the same class at school all our lives. And the teachers wouldn't like it. So it's really better to have fun now and then grow up just like other people.'

The end

And that is what happened.

Lapitch and Gita grew. Lapitch remained a shoemaker and Gita almost forgot that she had ever been in a circus. But once, something reminded her of it.

Some years later, a circus came to the town and Master Scowler took all of them to see it on Sunday.

Gita, sitting among the audience, saw a beautiful little girl come riding in on a white horse. The horse was Soko, just as good and gentle as he had always been. But he was even whiter than before because he had aged as horses do even though their troubles are not as great as those of men.

Gita also saw her parrot and learned that her bird and her horse were quite all right with the new circus boss. Soon after Gita had gone home with Lapitch, the old boss had fallen ill. But happily, he repented of his sins before he died.

When Gita and Lapitch were really grown up they married. Later, when Master Scowler was very old, Lapitch took over his business.

They had four children and three apprentices. And sometimes, on Sunday afternoons, the children and the apprentices would gather round to listen to the story of Lapitch's wonderful adventures.

His boots stood in a glass case, where everybody could see them.

And if anybody is sorry that we have come to the end of the story, he may read it again and count up all the people that Lapitch was able to help – because though he was small he was as cheerful as a bird, as brave as a knight, as wise as a book and as good as the sun.